Testimonies of Men and Women of Faith

IN THEIR OWN WORDS

BROADMAN & HOLMAN PUBLISHERS

NASHVILLE, TENNESSEE

TOM ELLIFF

ROBERT GEE WITTY

© 2003
by Thomas D. Elliff and Robert Gee Witty

All rights reserved
Printed in Canada

0-8054-2637-X

Published by Broadman & Holman Publishers
Nashville, Tennessee

Dewey Decimal Classification: 248.4
Subject Heading: CHRISTIAN LIFE—ANECDOTES \ CHRIST-
IAN BIOGRAPHY \ FAITH—ANECDOTES

Unless otherwise noted Scripture quotations are from the King
James Version or are the author's own paraphrase. Scripture quotations marked NKJV are from the New King James Version, copy-
right © 1979, 1980, 1982, Thomas Nelson, Inc., Publishers.

2 3 4 5 6 7 8 9 10   08 07 06 05 04 03

Yateli

IN THEIR OWN WORDS

119/10

Dedicated to
each of those individuals
whose testimonies appear in this book
with gratitude
for their conviction that
the Redeemed of the Lord
should "say so."
(Psalm 107:2)

TABLE OF CONTENTS

PROLOGUE:
IN THEIR OWN WORDS

By the time Marge* reached her assigned seat in the rear of the plane, she was crying openly. Mumbling apologetically, she stumbled over the passenger in the aisle seat, dropped heavily into her own, and turned toward the window where she was startled by the reflection of her tears. She hated it when she cried like this . . . and mentally added this weakness to the list of things she despised about herself.

How could he do this to her? After three years in a relationship she had seemingly held together with no help from him, he had dumped her—right out in front of the terminal, no less! Just a brief, "Look, Marge, this is not working. Let's quit fooling ourselves, and get on with our lives, OK? It's been great, but look, it's over. I wish you the best, kid." And with that he had slid behind the wheel. She had stood numbly, watching as his car was quickly absorbed in the traffic.

At first she had wanted to run after him. But then she thought better of it. "Not this time," she said to herself. "I can't take any more hurt and abuse."

1

So here she was, crying softly in the dim lights of the cabin as the plane climbed through the night sky. *I wish we'd just crash,* she thought to herself, and then added "Insensitivity to Others" to a lengthening list of things she didn't like about herself.

"Would you like a drink with your meal?" The flight attendant nudged Marge back into reality. "Uh, sure," Marge responded. "Ginger ale, please." Lowering her table, she turned to the window and slipped back into her despondent meditation.

What's the matter with me? she thought. *Why can't I ever get it right . . . maybe just once?* Subconsciously she retrieved the "pull-down menu" in her mind, which she kept for moments like this. *Things Done Wrong* was the title, and under it were subtitles that read, "Drugs and Sex in High School," "Pregnancy," "Abortion," "Dropout," "Hank," "Fired at IRP," "Charlie," "Argument with Dad and Mom," "Fred," "Three Years without Speaking to My Parents." Now she mentally typed in "Dumped by Jimmy" and sighed again. *Why can't I ever get it right?*

"Excuse me," said the man next to her. She had not even taken time to look at him until now. Spotting his worn wedding ring, she felt safer. But then she remembered that old geezer on the last flight and cautiously responded, "Yes . . . uh, what can I do for you?"

"Oh, nothing really," he said with a touch of weariness in his voice. "I was just wondering if I could do something for you."

Oh, boy, thought Marge, *and just when I thought I was safe!*

"You see," he continued, "I couldn't help but notice your tears. Family problem? Homesick? A death? Moving? Or none of the above?"

"Actually," replied Marge, "all of the above. But I don't feel like going there right now."

"I understand," said the stranger. Looking down at the sandwich that the attendant had plopped on both their trays, he said, "I'm going to pray over my meal. Is there something I can pray with you about?"

Marge was startled by that question. Caught off guard, she mumbled something like, "Pray I'll get it right just once in my life." Then she heard him prayerfully repeat that request as if he actually knew God personally.

The man slowly opened the meal container before asking, "May I tell you about an experience that revolutionized my life?"

"Why not?" Marge responded, actually wishing he would just let her be alone with her thoughts.

But then she found herself caught up in his brief account of what he called his "personal meeting with the Lord." She was especially interested in the result of that meeting: peace with God, power for living, and the confidence that he would live forever in heaven. Those were the things she so desperately wanted for herself.

"I'd give anything for that!" Marge surprised herself by musing out loud. She was equally surprised by his answer. "Oh, you don't have to give anything. You see, the price has already been paid."

As Marge gathered up her backpack, I handed her my business card, which she stuck inside the front cover of a well-worn novel.

3

"You know," she said with a contented smile, "I really do believe I have just done it right for the first time in my memory. I can't tell you what this means to me! And, by the way, I don't know if this makes any difference to you, but I have to tell you anyway. I've been to a few churches, sat in the back, and strained to hear the minister's sermon, which meant little to me. I really appreciate the fact that you took time to share . . . in your own words. That's made all the difference to me!"

Marge walked off the plane ahead of me and disappeared down the concourse. Watching her depart, I reflected on the remarkable power of God to change a life. I was taken by her statement: "You took time to share . . . in your own words."

You are invited on a brief journey through the pages of this book. In it you'll have the privilege of reading about people just like yourself—people who eagerly share about a remarkable, life-changing encounter with God . . . in their own words.

---

*For many years the authors have made a practice of asking others just how they might pray for them. "Marge" is a composite of many of the responses they have received to that question . . . and God's exciting answer to prayer.

4

I

ON TOP . . . BUT EMPTY

John Bisagno

One of life's biggest surprises is that it takes more than mere success to produce a full and meaningful life. Many people who would cringe at the thought of being down and out are rapidly filling the ranks of the "up and out." They have "arrived" professionally only to be haunted by a vague emptiness that still leaves them searching. True fulfillment will come only through a personal relationship with Christ. This was the discovery of John Bisagno.

As a nineteen-year-old jazz band leader, I was sitting on top of the world. I thought I had everything I would ever need to be happy: money, popularity, friends, and fun.

Soon I began to feel very empty. The thrill was gone, and

frustration was all I knew. On a lark, I accepted an invitation to attend the world's largest youth camp in Oklahoma.

Everyone there seemed to be truly happy—except me. Deeply stirred by the Holy Spirit the last night, I was the very first, among thousands, to respond to the invitation. At 9:01 P.M. August 1, 1952, Jesus came into my heart and changed everything. Nearly half a century has gone by, and today I love Him with a love that is as passionate and real as that very first moment.

The Bible speaks of a man much like John Bisagno—on top but empty. He was young, wealthy, and popular; a man of authority and seemingly impeccable moral credentials. His emptiness drove him to fall at the feet of Jesus and cry, "Good Master, what must I do to have eternal life?" Jesus reminded him that eternal life involved a choice—the choice to trust in Him alone. Will you make that choice?

"For what is a man profited, if he shall gain the whole world, and lose his own soul? or what shall a man give in exchange for his soul?" (Matt. 16:26).

2

SLAVES OF JESUS

Bill Bright
Vonette Bright

In April 1951, Bill and Vonette Bright signed a contract to become "slaves of Jesus." God has used this husband and wife union to impact the world for their Lord Jesus Christ with unique effectiveness, especially in evangelism. In their own words they tell how their incredible relationship with Christ began. First read Bill's testimony of faith in Christ.

In 1945 I received Jesus Christ into my life as Savior and Lord in response to my saintly mother's prayers, the ministry of Dr. Henrietta Mears, and the First Presbyterian Church of Hollywood.

In my youth I was a happy pagan. Influenced by Elmer Gantry, an unfaithful and immoral pastor, I had little to do with

7

the church through college, on the extension faculty of Oklahoma State University, and as a businessman in Hollywood.

On October 19, 2001, I will celebrate my eightieth birthday. To this very day no one has ever witnessed to me about my salvation. I received Christ alone on my knees in the privacy of my own home.

In 1948 Vonette and I were married and grew in our faith together. To know Jesus Christ of Nazareth is to love Him, and to love Him is to obey Him. In April 1951 Vonette and I signed a contract to become "slaves of Jesus," following His model (Phil. 2:7), the apostle Paul (Rom. 1:1), and the other apostles. Approximately twenty-four hours later God gave me a vision to help fulfill the Great Commission in my generation. The vision became Campus Crusade for Christ. The rest is history.

––––––––––––

Now read the testimony of Bill's wife, Vonette, who joined him in signing the contract to become "slaves of Jesus."

––––––––––––

I became a Christian as a result of trying to save Bill Bright from the influence of what I thought were overly religious people. Bill was in California, and I was in Texas at college. He encouraged me to come to California for a college briefing conference. We were very much in love and were engaged to be married, but we realized we were not in agreement on matters of faith. I had been offered teaching positions in Colorado and Oklahoma. However, I knew I had to go to California. If I could just spend time with Bill, I could convince him that it was all right to be religious, but you don't have to overdo it. My purpose was to see Bill Bright change his mind, or I would return his engagement ring and take a teaching position.

When I arrived in California, I met the most attractive, sharp, successful, young professionals I had ever seen. I was so surprised. I liked the way they looked and the quality of life they lived, but I didn't like what they said. They talked about God as if they knew Him personally. I didn't think that was possible. I had grown up in the church, and it meant a great deal to me, but I didn't know God personally. I thought their faith was just new to them, and one day they would get back to normal.

After the conference I decided that this was right for Bill's life, but I knew this would not work for me. Bill suggested we go talk to Dr. Henrietta Mears, Christian education director at Hollywood Presbyterian Church. She had taught chemistry in Minneapolis, and since I had majored in chemistry, she spoke with me in scientific terms. She shared with me, for the first time to my understanding, that God loved me and had a plan for my life, that He wanted me to live an abundant life. The reason I could not know God's love and plan for my life was because of sin. She told me that God had sent His Son, Jesus, to pay the penalty for my sin, and it's through Him that we can know God's love and plan. I realized I had nothing to lose and everything in the world to gain if what she said was true. Though I thought I was a Christian, I wasn't sure. Dr. Mears encouraged me to make sure by inviting Jesus Christ into my life, to trust Him, and to believe in Him according to John 1:12.

I point back to that experience as the time when my life began to change. I found some areas in my life that I hadn't been able to control, God began to control and handled beautifully. The Bible became a living book, and prayers seemed to go above the ceiling. I was experiencing God's direction. I found myself as enthusiastic as the people who had influenced my husband. That was fifty-three years ago, and the reality of God has grown greater with every year.

Do you have Jesus in your heart? Would you like to have Jesus come into your life? Let me encourage you to ask Him into your heart right now.

Millions of people have read Bill Bright's tract, "The Four Spiritual Laws." The first law speaks to the fact of God's love for you. Have you come to experience that love through a personal faith in Christ?

"A servant of Jesus Christ, called to be an apostle,
separated unto the gospel of God" (Rom. 1:1).

3

NEVER TOO SOON!

Truett Cathy

Some people doubt that a child can have a genuine experience with God. Jesus said that we all must come to Him in childlike faith "for of such is the kingdom of God." Truett Cathy, founder of Chick-fil-A, expresses gratitude that his life-changing encounter came at an early age.

At age eight I started in the restaurant business and met my wife, Jeannette. At age twelve I received Jesus Christ as my Savior and Lord. This is not to say that I have always lived up to God's expectations. But I do thank the Lord that I have not done a lot of things that I would have done had I not invited Jesus Christ into my heart at an early age. It seems God steered me in the proper direction very early, preparing me for the position I now hold. God has bestowed many, many blessings on my life: a wonderful wife for fifty-four years, three wonderful children, twelve natural grandchildren, and one hundred twenty-five grandchildren by choice.

I have also been blessed with an exciting business, Chick-fil-A, which is approaching one thousand restaurants and generating over one billion dollars per year in sales. Because of my success in business, all my financial needs have been met, plus I have been allowed the joy of giving to many people and seeing the benefits derived from these gifts.

Thanks be to God, for His wonderful gift of life and life abundantly, even into eternity.

———————

What if you did not come to Christ at an early age? The Bible has a message for you: "Now is the day of salvation!"

"From a child thou hast known the holy scriptures,
which are able to make thee wise unto salvation through
faith which is in Christ Jesus" (2 Tim. 3:15).

4

WHEN THE BLIND LED THE BLIND

Morris Chapman

Giving leadership to the world's largest evangelical denomination is an incredibly demanding responsibility. How important it must be to have the daily assurance of God's strength and a clear sense of vision. Yet there was a time when Morris Chapman was spiritually blind. Interestingly, God used another blind man to point him to the light of the world.

My life's story begins before I was born. After five years of marriage, my parents had no children. My mother was thirty-one years of age and desperately wanted to have a child. Like Hannah of the Old Testament (1 Sam. 1:9–20), my mother prayed a vow to the Lord that if He would give her a child, she would give him to the Lord. In the sixth year of my parents' marriage, her first of two sons was born. She never forgot her vow to lead her son in the ways of the Lord. Neither did she mention to me the vow of her prayer until I was in the eleventh grade in high school, long after I sensed God calling me into Christian vocational ministry at the age of twelve. She had the wisdom and patience to wait upon the Lord until in His time he called me to the ministry. To this day I am grateful for godly parents.

Faithful to her promise, Mother did not simply send me to church. She and Dad took me to church, a practice they continued until I left for college. Week after week I was in church learning the powerful truths of the Bible in Sunday school, Vacation Bible School, Royal Ambassadors, and congregational worship.

The reality that a life can be radically changed at any age is a miracle of God. I continue to be amazed that God spoke to the heart of this seven-year-old in such a simple, yet profound way. I am even more amazed that I understood the need to ask forgiveness of my sins and invite Christ into my life. As a young Mississippi boy, I was born into the kingdom of God. I became His child! By the promise of His Word, I shall forever remain one of His.

My conversion to Christ happened in the midst of a revival meeting under the preaching of an anointed evangelist and the singing of an inspiring gospel singer. While the preaching of the evangelist touched me, God used the singing and piano playing of the blind gospel singer to captivate my heart. Throughout the week I was overwhelmed with the thought of how great God must be. He had wonderfully blessed this talented musician and was using him mightily to testify to the saving power of Jesus' name. In this setting the Holy Spirit revealed to me God's truth and my need, and I trusted Jesus with my whole heart.

I will never forget making known to my parents my desire to accept Jesus as my personal Savior. Wisely, they made an appointment with our pastor. He opened God's Word and lovingly led me through the scriptural steps to salvation. In his office I prayed for God to forgive my sins, and I professed my belief in Jesus as my Savior. The following Sunday morning, during the invitation, I stepped into the aisle of the church and walked to the altar to publicly profess my faith in Jesus Christ.

That night I followed Him obediently in believer's baptism, a portrait of the death, burial, and resurrection of Jesus. My baptism also was an outward symbol of my inward conversion, a picture of my sins having been washed away by the shed blood of Jesus, my burial with Him in baptism, and my having been raised to walk in newness of life.

That week was a glorious and miraculous time for me. Thank the Lord I have never been the same. I live victoriously, my sins covered by the blood of the Lamb. I live with the assurance that one day I will be face-to-face with Jesus. Praise His holy name.

God uses many means of introducing people to the simple fact that, in Jesus, they can have eternal life. Have you responded to that Good News? Have you taken time to express gratitude to God for those who showed you the way?

15

In Their Own Words

"Philip findeth Nathanael, and saith unto him, We have found him, of whom Moses in the law, and the prophets, did write, Jesus of Nazareth" (John 1:45).

5

TWINS WATCH MOM
J. R. Church

Here is a remarkable example of the effective ministry of a Christian woman who took the time to teach children. Now you can read how J. R. Church and his twin brother, Terry, heard the gospel with other children who crowded into the living room of their teacher. There they learned of Jesus' love, enjoyed singing simple, happy songs, came to believe in prayer, and prayed the sinner's prayer. Their life-changing experience came to a happy climax as their mother joined them in baptism.

I grew up in Lubbock, a community in west Texas, at the heart of the "caprock"—the largest area on the face of the planet. There were few tall trees around Lubbock because of the dry climate. In fact, most trees leaned slightly to the east and northeast because of the constant wind.

Our neighborhood was average for the 1940s. Dad had designed and built our modest home himself. The streets around our area were not paved when we moved there. As my twin brother and I grew up, our neighborhood grew up with us. I remember watching the construction as streets were paved, houses were built, businesses appeared, and a junior high school covered the vacant acreage half a block west of our house.

The children in our neighborhood were great friends. Terry and I had a big sister, a big brother, a dog, friends, and two parents who loved us very much.

When I was seven years old, a neighbor friend invited us to attend a Wednesday afternoon neighborhood Bible class. He said he would get a prize for every guest he could bring. Well, he got a bargain with me! I had a twin!

The Bible teacher lived just two blocks south, an easy walk down Avenue P. We lived on Thirty-First Street, three houses east of Avenue P., and Mrs. Pauline Click's house was on the corner of Thirty-Third and Avenue P. About thirty children crowded into her living room, sitting on the floor, couch, and every chair she had. She had set up a flannel graph board next to her piano. Her daughter led in the singing of children's songs as Mrs. Click accompanied her on the piano. Those songs quickly became my favorites—"Do Lord," "Jesus Loves Me," "I'm in the Lord's Army"—the simple songs of the 1940s.

Every week Mrs. Click would teach the class a memory verse. I think her favorite verse was, "Thy word have I hid in mine heart, that I might not sin against thee" (Ps. 119:11). For the next eight years I would be attending that class every Wednesday afternoon after school, memorizing Scripture verses.

That first day I heard her teach about the "Telephone to Heaven." The phone number was J-E-S-U-S. Mom was very sick at the time, so after the class I asked her to give me that number again. I needed to talk to God about my mom. What is so amazing about prayer is that God heard every prayer I prayed as a child. I cannot remember Him not answering every one.

My heart was ready. At the end of each lesson, she would invite the children who had never been saved to receive Jesus into their hearts. Not long after we began to attend, my brother and I responded. We stood together . . . she sat on her couch. She explained that all were born with a sin nature because of Adam and Eve. His sin brought death to mankind. But we could obtain eternal life by simply asking Jesus to forgive and save us.

Both Terry and I bowed our heads and prayed a simple sinner's prayer: "Dear Jesus, I know that I am a sinner and that You died to pay my sin debt. Please forgive me of my sins. Come into my heart and save me. I pray in Jesus' name. Amen."

From that day to this, I know that I have eternal life. Though Mrs. Click was a Presbyterian, she never insisted that we attend her church. But when some neighbors began to take Terry and me to a denominational church that she did not approve of, she had a talk with Mom. At her encouragement Terry and I were taken to a Baptist church where at ten years old, we were baptized—arm in arm—together. Then we moved to one side of the baptistry and watched as Mom was baptized that same night.

Armed with a "Wordless Book," I began to tell our neighborhood friends about Jesus. The black page stood for sin. The red page stood for the blood of Christ. The white page stood for our sins being forgiven. The gold page stood for heaven, and the green cover stood for Christian growth. I was so excited about heaven and eternal life that I just kept winning children. In the fifth grade, I wrote the names of twenty-five children in the back of my New Testament as I won them to the Lord.

I always knew that God wanted me to serve Him. I preached my first sermon at seven years old, standing on a chair behind the pulpit of a small church. My text was John 3:16! I was born to be a preacher.

Often you read of the impact of a praying mother. Here you have read of the influence of a praying child. Do you have a father or mother who needs your prayers?

"And it shall be, if He calls you, that you must say, 'Speak, LORD, for Your servant hears'" (1 Sam. 3:9 NKJV).

6

FINDING CHRIST IN CHURCH

Forrest Claunch
William Crews
William Wayne Bennett, Jr.

Often Jesus will confront people in a synagogue or in the temple. Here are three testimonies of people who met Christ in church.

Forrest Claunch met Christ in Sunday school.

My sister Mary, four years my senior, took me along with her to Sunday school and most of the time to worship, when I was seven years old. We never saw our parents in church, but they did not mind our attendance.

It was the faithful and patient work and witness of Sunday school teachers and the pastor, Kring Allen, that brought me to understand my need of a Savior and that Jesus Christ was the only one who could save me. In April 1953 I made that decision and was baptized.

As a thirteen-year-old boy I did not know much, but those years of Sunday school, worship services, Vacation Bible School, and fellowship times were used by the Holy Spirit to convict me of sin and convince me of salvation by God the Father through Jesus Christ His Son.

William Bennett met Christ in a revival service.

As a preteen I was saved in a revival meeting. My basic motivation was to escape hell and go to heaven, but as I walked out of the church, I remember the words "whiter than snow, yes, whiter than snow. Now wash me, and I shall be whiter than snow." There must have been a sense of forgiveness as well as relief on missing hell and going to heaven.

Since that time there have been numerous rededications in my life. I continue to battle the old nature and look forward to being free from the presence of sin in heaven.

William (Bill) Crews met Christ in a worship service.

My earliest recollection is sitting at my mother's feet while she held my baby sister and sang gospel songs in the small Baptist church across the street from our little home. When the pastor preached, my mother read Bible stories to me and my baby sister.

At age seven I received Jesus as my Savior through the witness of my parents, my Sunday school teacher, and my best friend, the pastor's son of the new church plant in our community. At age thirteen, I felt called to the gospel ministry, preached my first sermon at age fifteen, and was called to be pastor of my first church at age seventeen.

The church has always been influential in my Christian journey. Every good thing in my life has resulted from the ministry of a local church. Consequently, like Jesus, I love the church.

––––––––––

It is not so much *where* you have met Christ as *whether* you have met Him. Have you?

"And daily in the temple, and in every house, they ceased not to teach and preach Jesus Christ" (Acts 5:42).

7

BROKEN NECK, BLESSED LIFE

YoYo Collins

For many people a minor handicap becomes an excuse to blame God and to escape any responsibility to serve others. In his own words, YoYo Collins tells how a diving accident put his paralyzed body in a wheelchair but brought such a reality to the love of God that he and his wife were liberated to an inspiring ministry that challenges thousands.

Mom began taking my brother, sister, and me to church here in Salina when I was very young. We went to the Methodist church when we lived next door to it (when I was about five). And we began going to First Baptist Church when I was about seven or eight. One Sunday morning when I was nine, God, the Holy Spirit, spoke to my heart to make me know how unclean we all are in our

24

sin, how personally unclean I was inside, and that Christ could cleanse me and save me. To me, accepting Christ, inviting Him into my life, was just the best and sensible thing to do . . . so I did it! Thank God for childlike thinking, for childlike faith! No matter how old we become, that's how we must come to Christ.

I remember very vividly knowing the absolute cleansing of my total being by the Holy Spirit. For a time, and because God helped me to begin to understand the sacrifice Jesus had made for me, all my thoughts and actions were consumed by what would please God. I remember saying to myself, *I must stop thinking those thoughts,* or *I must stop doing that,* or *I need to start doing these things. God has saved me forever, and I owe everything to Him.*

In my teenage years I thought I was doing all right without God, drifting into absolute disregard for what He wanted to do in my life. But in 1977, after ten years of trying to move away from God, I broke my neck in a diving accident that left me paralyzed from the collarbone down, permanently confined to a wheelchair.

God used that accident, and the "state of arrest" that the paralysis had placed me in, to show me that He had always been with me. God showed me that He cared very much about my condition and my future. He gave me a wonderful helpmate in my precious wife, Sandi. And He has allowed us to serve Him in the itinerate ministry He gave us in 1980. We've shared in nearly two hundred churches, conferences, and conventions each year since Sandi resigned her teaching position to go into full-time ministry in

1982. His provision has been immeasurable throughout our lives. What a mighty God we serve!

It is so easy to murmur, "I can't." One man said his mother taught him to knock the *t* out of *can't*. What are you doing with your handicap? Have you turned it over to Christ?

"And he said unto me, My grace is sufficient for thee: for my strength is made perfect in weakness. Most gladly therefore will I rather glory in my infirmities, that the power of Christ may rest upon me" (2 Cor. 12:9).

8

THE "HATCHET MAN"

Charles Colson

He was up!

He was down!

He is now really up!

But you must let Charles Colson tell his own amazing story of a crushing and shameful fall and an incredible new life of respect, service, and national challenge.

My life was the American dream fulfilled—grandson of immigrants, first person in my family to go to college, youngest company officer in the Marine Corps, youngest administrative assistant in the United States Senate, successful lawyer, and at age thirty-seven, seated in the office next to the President of the United States.

As special counsel to the president, I was in and out of his office daily, one of a handful of men who made the great decisions affecting our country. But in late 1972, after President Nixon's landslide reelection victory, I prepared to leave the White House and return to my law office. At that very moment, a great scandal called Watergate was emerging, and soon I found myself caught in its grip, under investigation by congressional committees and prosecutors. My world of power, pride, and possessions was collapsing.

In the midst of it all, I renewed an old friendship. Now practicing law, I returned to the Raytheon Company, one of the largest corporations in America, to be its counsel, and spent time with Tom Phillips, its president. I was struck by how different Tom was from the man I had known four years before. He was calm, peaceful, interested in me.

In the summer of 1973, he told me what had happened to him, that Jesus Christ had come into his life, that he had found meaning and purpose, and for the first time in his life, he was at peace with himself. It was a beautiful story he recounted to me, along with reading from the wonderful little book entitled *Mere Christianity,* written by one of the intellectual giants of the twentieth century, C. S. Lewis. I left Tom's house that night barely able to hold my emotions in check. And that evening, in my automobile in his driveway—the toughest of the Nixon tough guys, the White House hatchet man and ex-Marine captain—I found myself crying too hard to drive the car out of the driveway. I called out to God, asking Him to change my life, to take me the way I was.

From that night to today, my life was dramatically changed. It will never be the same again; it never can be. I live each day in the deepest gratitude to God that on the cross of Calvary two thousand years ago, the Son of God died to take away *my* sins. I am so overwhelmed by that one act of history that I will spend the rest of my days serving Christ.

Following my experience in prison for a Watergate offense, I have devoted my life to working with prisoners. Today the ministry of Prison Fellowship is in eighty-eight countries of the world, bringing the gospel to thousands upon thousands of prisoners in need. It was a thrill flying on Air Force One, traveling with the president, and hearing the band play "Hail to the Chief." But the thrill I had in those days pales in significance to the thrill I have in my ministry, seeing God transform the lives of the lost and give hope to the hopeless. When we serve Christ by taking the gospel to others, we think we're blessing them; the real truth is God is blessing us.

———————

There is no reasonable explanation for the amazing changes in the status of this international personality except one: God. Have you ever come to a point in your life when you said, "Only God can help me!"?

"Seek ye the LORD while he may be found, call ye upon him while he is near: Let the wicked forsake his way, and the unrighteous man his thoughts: and let him return unto the LORD, and he will have mercy upon him; and to our God, for he will abundantly pardon" (Isa. 55:6—7).

9

THE BOY WHO KNEW HIS DESTINY

W. A. Criswell

One of the most important questions that anyone can answer is, Why am I here? or, What is my purpose in life? Now you can read in his own words that W. A. Criswell knew at a very early age that God planned for him to be a preacher. The testimony of this honored pastor records the story that reaches back into his boyhood experience with the Lord Jesus Christ.

"Do you love the Lord, son?" the young pastor from Dalhart asked me as we sat in the kitchen drinking fresh buttermilk and eating my mother's oatmeal-raisin cookies, still warm from the oven.

"Yes, sir," I answered honestly.

Pastor John Hicks had come to Texline from Dalhart, the county seat, to hold our annual revival. It was an honor to have the evangelist stay with our family for the weeklong duration of the meetings. There were services every morning at 10:00 and every evening at 7:30. Pastor Hicks was young. His sermons were exciting. They made me laugh and cry. I was just ten years old, but I remember that he treated me like a man, and I admired him like teenagers today admire movie stars and singers.

"So you like Zane Gray stories, do you?" Pastor Hicks asked with a grin. "Me too!" he said before I could even smile or nod in reply. "But don't tell my deacons," he added. "They think Southern Baptist preachers should stick to Matthew, Mark, Luke, and John."

He laughed heartily and poured another glass of buttermilk.

"Your mother tells me that you're going to be a doctor like your grandfather," he said, wiping the foamy white buttermilk from his mustache.

"No, sir," I answered. "I'm going to be a preacher."

Pastor Hicks leaned over conspiratorially and whispered. "Why's that, boy? Preaching means hard work and no pay. Doctors make loads of money."

I was surprised by his reply until I realized by the gleam in his eyes that he was teasing me.

"I don't care," I answered. "I want to be a preacher, and that's that."

I'm sure that desire came directly from God, but just when it started or exactly why I'm still not sure. I just know that even before I was saved, the Lord planted it deep in my heart that I would be a pastor—not an evangelist, not a missionary, but a pastor. My father didn't want me to be a preacher. My mother

31

didn't want me to be a preacher. But somehow I knew that in spite of everything and everybody, a preacher I would be.

The Wednesday morning revival service was held in our little Southern Baptist church at exactly the same time I was supposed to be in school. But my mother was glad to write an excuse, which I delivered to our principal. I arrived at the revival service ten or fifteen minutes late and sneaked into a pew directly behind my mother. Pastor Hicks winked at me as he stood to preach.

I don't remember what he read from the Bible that day or what he preached about. I was sitting there listening with all my heart when slowly it dawned upon me that this was the day I would accept Christ as my personal Lord and Savior. By the time the sermon ended, tears were running down my cheeks. I was only ten. I hadn't murdered anybody, and I wasn't a hardened criminal, but I did have a growing conviction that this was my day to enter Christ's glorious kingdom.

> There is a fountain filled with blood,
> Drawn from Emmanuel's veins.
> And sinners plunged beneath that flood
> Lose all their guilty stains.

The pastor's wife had adjusted the piano stool and was playing that great old hymn of invitation. The little congregation made up mostly of women and little children sang heartily. Pastor Hicks was leaning against the pulpit, his head bowed and his eyes closed in prayer. Suddenly my mother turned in her pew and leaned down to speak to me.

"Son, today will you accept Christ as your Lord and Savior?"

I looked up at her. My heart was pounding with excitement. Today would mark the end of one life and the beginning of another.

"W. A." she whispered, "will you give your heart to Christ today?"

"Yes, Mother," I said. "I will."

She smiled and nodded as I left my seat and walked alone to the front of the church. Pastor Hicks came down from the pulpit to greet me, but I couldn't even see him through my tears. I was a child, but I was so deeply moved by that moment. I was being born again. I was being saved. I was inviting Christ into my heart to rule my life forever. I was entering His kingdom, the kingdom of God. I was becoming a Christian. It felt wonderful. I was happy, but I was crying like a baby. And Mother told me later that everybody in the church was crying with me.

The next thing I knew, the pastor of our church in Texline, Brother L. S. Hill, was standing beside me addressing the tiny congregation.

"Today, this young boy, W. A. Criswell, Jr., stands before you accepting the Lord Jesus as his Savior and requesting to be baptized into the fellowship of the church. All of you who are in favor of receiving him on his confession of faith as a candidate for baptism, please raise your hand."

Every hand in the place shot up. Pastor Hill smiled and closed the service with a benediction. And every man, woman, and child in the little Texline Southern Baptist church lined up to shake my hand, to pat my head, to tell me how happy I had made them, and to welcome me officially into the body of Christ.

Can you give a clear and assured answer to the questions that Criswell faced as a boy? Do you know your relationship with Christ? Do you know your purpose in life? Are you fulfilling your destiny? You can through Christ Jesus.

"But when it pleased God, who separated me from my mother's womb, and called me by his grace, to reveal his Son in me, that might preach him" (Gal. 1:15–16a).

Testimony taken from W. A. Criswell, *Standing on the Promises,* Nashville: Tenn., 1990. All rights reserved.

34

10

BRANDED ... THEN BORN AGAIN

Daniel Davis, Jr.

It is a fact that many people become deeply committed to a particular brand of religion long before they come to a point of personal salvation. Chaplain (Colonel) Daniel O. Davis, Jr., USA (retired), is such an individual. Having sought to introduce men and women to Christ from the rice paddies of Vietnam to the desert sands of Operation Desert Storm, he writes of the positive impact of his "brand" of religion and of the necessity of being born again.

In 1932 in a small, quiet central Florida town called Orlando, I first saw the light of day. My dear mother was a young woman from Ohio who had committed her life in marriage to my gallant, youthful father who got his start in south Georgia.

The Davis Clan of which I am a part was largely centered in Kershaw County, South Carolina. In the beginning years of the twentieth century, my paternal grandfather began looking beyond "life on the farm" for what he would consider to be better opportunities. He loaded up his fledgling family and made his way down through Georgia to settle, once and for all, in Orlando, Florida.

As I was growing up, I was introduced to our "brand" of religion. Our particular group of Davises is primarily Baptist with a strong strain of Methodism very much alive within our ranks. Basic religion among our people calls for honor and respect for the living God and His Word and for the acknowledgement of Jesus Christ as the Son of God, humanity's only Savior. There is no doubting the fact that Jesus Christ died on the cross of Calvary as a fit and proper sacrifice for the sins of humanity and that He arose from the grave on the third day. We also look for the coming of Christ again from heaven.

A strong practical commitment to biblical teachings and principles as well as a high regard for the local church is a hallmark for our people. We honor God and parents. We are loyal to family and friends, and we treat others fairly. We go to church, we read the Bible, we believe in a literal heaven and hell. Our lifestyle says that we are good, God-fearing people.

We fully believe that at some point in life, every individual needs to repent of sin and to trust Jesus Christ as personal Savior and Lord. We hold to a deep-seated belief that this personal salvation is extremely important before death claims the individual.

But as important as personal conversion to Christ may be to us, we are hardly given to evangelistic urgency. Hopefully, in God's good time, the individual will experience salvation and thereby escape eternal damnation. But the practice of personally leading others to Christ is not entered into by most of our people. We go to great lengths to get people to attend church, revival meetings, and other evangelistic activities, but we leave soul-winning to the preacher, the evangelist, and others who may have been called of God for such efforts.

For as long as I can remember, this brand of religion has, more or less, held an important place in my life. When I was a child, my mother taught me the various biblical stories and songs about Jesus that were usually taught to children of that time. As a small boy I started attending Sunday school and church worship, primarily at the Lucerne Park Baptist Church in Orlando, Florida. Vacation Bible School was usually an exciting part of my summers. Scriptural memory verses were important. I could quote John 3:16 long before I had any idea of what the verse really meant.

It was through these church-centered activities that the Word of God began to "take hold" in my young life. I came under the convicting power of the Holy Spirit at a tender age, and by the time I was ten years old, I knew that I was a lost and dying sinner, separated from God. My parents and grandparents, along with Sunday school teachers and other Christian workers, took the time to teach me about Jesus and His Word. But I cannot remember a single time that any one of them ever took me aside to make a try at personal evangelism, to urge me personally to give my heart to Jesus. They believed that if I was kept under the preaching and teaching of the Bible, in due time I would be led by the preacher or someone else to confess Christ as my Savior. God would see to it.

The series of pastors who served our church were, without exception, men of God. I remember that they were all conservative Bible preachers who never failed to plead for people to give their hearts and lives to Jesus Christ. From the time that I was about ten years of age to the time that I was thirteen, there were few worship services in which I did not struggle with God about surrendering to Jesus. I attended every service fully expecting to have to wrestle with God about the matter.

The years slipped by, and the convicting work of the Holy Spirit in my life became more and more powerful. The heavy load on my shoulders seemed almost to weigh me down. It was the load of sin not forgiven, a load made even heavier by my refusal of God's mercy extended to me. There were times when I felt that my heart would explode with God's conviction of sin. I would dream of being lost in hell, of being separated from Christ for all eternity. Time and time again I would think of the return of Jesus for His church. It struck fear in my heart to anticipate that blessed event because I knew that if He did come I would be left behind. In the heart of God, my salvation was an urgent matter; but in my own sinful heart, such was not the case.

Finally the day came when I could no longer resist God. Under the biblical preaching of my faithful pastor and in answer to his persistent invitation, at thirteen years of age, I surrendered my heart and life to Jesus Christ. I walked the aisle of the Lucerne Park Baptist Church, took my pastor by the hand, and listened carefully as he led me to open my heart and to receive Jesus Christ as my Savior and Lord. The moment I said yes to Jesus, in tender mercy He forgave my sin, lifted the heavy load from my shoulders, set me free from fear, and filled my heart with His love and presence. My life has never been the same. There has never been a day that I have doubted my salvation and the presence of the Holy Spirit within. I am on my way to heaven.

Approximately a year later God spoke to my heart and called me to preach. I finally surrendered to that call as a young man twenty-two years of age. For forty-eight years I have preached the unsearchable riches of the gospel of Christ. Thirty of those years were served as a chaplain to the men, women, and families of the United States Army. From the rice paddies of Vietnam to the desert sands of Operation Desert Storm, it has been my calling, my privilege, and my pleasure to preach the gospel of Christ to a pluralistic society with a sense of evangelistic fervor and urgency. All glory and honor to the living God.

I am still very much a part of the Davis Clan out of Kershaw County, South Carolina. Our brand of religion has enabled me to stand resolutely for God and His Word in the various circumstances of life. But every effort has been made to alter our perceptions with reference to the matters of personally practicing soul-winning, adhering to the urgency of the gospel, and being actively involved in leading people to receive God's salvation as early in life as possible. Today is the day of salvation; today is God's good time to be saved. "To day if ye will hear his voice, harden not your hearts" (Heb. 3:15).

Jesus constantly reminded His followers that mere religion was not sufficient to guarantee eternal life. Do you have a personal relationship with Christ—or only an empty religion?

"Many will say to me in that day, Lord, Lord, have we not prophesied in thy name? and in thy name have cast out devils? and in thy name done many wonderful works? And then will I profess unto them, I never knew you: depart from me, ye that work iniquity"
(Matt. 7:22–23).

II

Turning Hearts Toward Home

James Dobson, Jr.
Shirley Dobson

Think of the daily miracle of focusing the attention of worldwide millions on building the family. You will think of one man, James Dobson. Think of the miracle of focusing America on a National Day of Prayer. You will think of one woman, Shirley Dobson. Now you can read in their own words how this remarkable family began and continued their spiritual journey.

James Dobson tells us:

After I was grown, my parents told me that I had attempted to pray even before I learned to talk. I was imitating the sounds I had

41

heard from around the family altar. Two years later, at three years old, I made a conscious decision to become a Christian. You may think it is impossible for a child that young to make friends with Jesus, but it happened. I remember the occasion clearly today.

I was attending a Sunday evening church service and was sitting near the back with my mother. My father was the pastor, and at the end of his sermon, he invited people to come forward and give their hearts to the Lord. Fifteen or twenty men and women stepped into the aisle, and I joined them spontaneously. I recall kneeling at the altar and asking Jesus to come into my heart. I cried and asked Him to forgive my sins, whatever they had been in my first three years. That memory is still very tender in my mind today. Imagine the King of the universe, Creator of all heaven and earth, caring about an insignificant kid barely out of toddlerhood! I knew that He had heard me, and I felt so clean inside.

After the service my parents went to visit some members and left me in the car. As I sat there alone, I remember thinking about what I had done and what it really meant. The decision I made on that night has shaped all the intervening years of my life.

Now read Shirley Dobson's testimony.

As many of my friends know, and as I've written and shared a number of times, I had a very difficult childhood. Our family was dysfunctional because of my father's drinking, and unfortunately my parents' marriage ended in divorce when I was twelve. In the midst of the turmoil, my loving mother looked for a source of help that would bring a measure of stability into the lives of my brother and me. Sensing our neighborhood evangelical church was a place of refuge and hope, Mom made certain that we attended services, even though she couldn't always accompany us.

I listened to the Sunday school lessons each week and was introduced to Jesus; soon I knelt at an altar of prayer to ask Him into my heart. My life was changed forever when this little girl who felt like a "nobody" came to know her heavenly Father who loved her and called her by name! As my relationship with Christ grew, so did my prayer life. Each night I would kneel by my bed, asking the Lord to heal my family and pouring out my concerns to Him. Seeing God at work in the situations I brought to Him, I received faith-building affirmation that He hears and answers when His children pray.

Through the years daily prayer has continued to be my anchor. Little could I have foreseen, however, that the youngster who softly prayed in her darkened room long ago would be given the remarkable privilege of serving as chairman of the National Day of Prayer. This opportunity has allowed me to share my belief in Jesus Christ and the power of prayer with millions of Americans. I'm filled with gratitude as I reflect on how the Lord has helped me to overcome my past and led me in His truth. He is good, and I am confident that He stands ready to meet the needs of *all* who come to Him, doing "immeasurably more than we ask or imagine" (Eph. 3:20).

In Their Own Words

James and Shirley Dobson will tell you that the one essential for a successful family is faith in Christ. Has your family experienced Christ's life-changing power?

"Choose you this day whom ye will serve . . . but as for me and my house, we will serve the LORD" (Josh. 24:15).

12

FINDING HEAVEN ON THE BACK PORCH

James T. Draper, Jr.

Jimmy Draper is head of one of the largest religious publishing enterprises in the United States. Convicted of sin, he met Christ on the back porch of a parsonage in a small Arkansas town. What his experience may lack in drama, it makes up for in the difference he sensed when he received Christ.

I was born into the home of a Southern Baptist pastor who had married the daughter of a Southern Baptist pastor. So both my father and maternal grandfather were Southern Baptist pastors. I was born in the parsonage at Hartford, Arkansas, on October 10, 1935. My father was pastor of the First Baptist Church there. When I was eighteen months old, my family moved to Fort Worth, Texas, where my father enrolled in Southwestern Baptist

Theological Seminary. After three years there and the graduation of my father, we moved to Clarksville, Arkansas, where my father was pastor of the First Baptist Church.

All of my life I had heard the gospel message, and I grew up in a loving atmosphere with consistent Christian conduct on the part of my parents. Since I am the oldest of three sons, I had my mother's undivided attention for the first six and one-half years of my life. As I neared my sixth birthday, the Lord began to deal with my heart and began to reveal to me my need of the Savior. All of this came to a climax when my mother and I traveled to another town in Arkansas for the last weekend of a revival my father was preaching there. On Saturday night of that revival, the Lord really convicted me of my need to be saved. I even turned to another young boy sitting by me and said to him during the invitation, "I'll go if you will."

Neither of us moved forward at that time, but I could not get away from the conviction. I remember that we were staying with the pastor's family in the parsonage. I was sleeping on a screened-in back porch. When it was bedtime, I began to weep as I talked with my mother and dad and told them I knew I was a sinner and needed to be saved. That night on the back porch of the parsonage in a small town in Arkansas, I received Jesus Christ as my Savior.

My parents did not push me into baptism, waiting until the Lord revealed to me what I needed to do. I was nearly nine years old when I made a public profession of faith and was baptized, but I have never doubted that I was saved that night just before my sixth birthday on the back porch of a parsonage.

I have often thought that my testimony isn't dramatic or sensational, but throughout my life I have been grateful to God that He saved me from a lot of things and not out of them. I have also rejoiced in the truth that I needed to be saved just as much as the oldest, most visible sinner in the world! Each of us is separated from God and needs to be saved whenever God moves in our hearts.

———————

Jimmy Draper's testimony is a reminder that all of us must come to Christ in simple faith and repentance. Have you?

"Trust in the LORD with all your heart, and lean not on your own understanding; in all your ways acknowledge Him, and He shall direct your paths" (Prov. 3:5–6 NKJV).

13

INFLUENCE
Jim Elliff

If you meet Jim Elliff today, he could tell you of at least fifteen preachers who are descendants of his great-grandfather. Yet Jim Elliff had to meet Christ on God's terms. Jim was not only influenced by his family heritage; he has become an influencer to thousands, turning their hearts to Christ.

My great-grandfather was converted on a train outside of Little Rock, Arkansas, just after the death of his godly wife on that very train. Much of his life had been lived in disobedience to God. But God can save the years of a man as well as his soul, and we therefore hope that the future generations of converts coming from a new believer will not have to experience years of rebellion toward God before conversion. That is exactly what happened to my great-grandfather's descendants.

I was only nine years of age when I felt the conviction of the Spirit. Like most children in sincere Christian homes, I was exposed to Christ throughout my growing-up days. My knowledge of Bible facts was not sufficient to convert me. Those truths I had learned from my parents and from Sunday school teachers were important, however, because we have to believe truths about Christ before we can put our full or implicit faith in Christ. I learned the nature of my sin, that Christ was the perfect substitute for my sin, and that I could not become a true Christian on my own merit. My only hope was to come to Christ by putting my full trust in Him alone for my salvation.

During a series of evangelistic meetings at the Bethany Baptist Church in Kansas City, Missouri, in 1957, I was confronted with the gospel in a way that the Holy Spirit made so appealing and so convincing that I could not resist any longer. I went home in the car with my mother and siblings that evening feeling like I had a thick, wet overcoat of conviction on my shoulders. My mother was willing to talk it over with me in her bedroom. She explained the story of Christ's death for sinners one more time. I saw it all and believed. Kneeling down, I prayed about my condition and asked God to save me.

I am fully satisfied that He did justify me that hour. Unlike many I have only had a brief period of doubt about the effect of that evening with God. My pastor father was away from home that night with the visiting evangelist. I gave my first witness to that conversion to my father over the phone in a way that was not at all profound, but certainly heartfelt, by saying with tears, "Dad, I sure am happy." My witness has matured, but that well of happiness has not dried up. My subsequent call to preach and all the thousands of preached and written messages, plus untold scores of personal evangelistic encounters, began that evening by my mother's bed.

Most of us can think of others whom God has used to turn our hearts toward Christ. Have you taken the time to thank God for these people whom He has used to influence your life?

"Therefore said I unto you, that no man can come unto me, except it were given unto him of my Father" (John 6:65).

50

14

BEYOND FORGIVENESS

Elisabeth Elliot

It is the rare person who has not heard the story of Jim Elliot, a missionary martyred by the Auca Indians to whom he had come as a witness for Christ. Remarkably his wife, Elisabeth, reached beyond forgiveness to those same Indians, leading them to faith in Christ. You can read in her own words where Elisabeth became so firmly grounded in her faith.

I grew up in a thoroughly Christian home. Each morning my father rose at five o'clock in order to meet with the Lord. When he came to breakfast at seven, we were aware that he had been on his knees in prayer. Following breakfast we went to the living room, sang a hymn (all the stanzas!—one hymn per day), then our father read the Bible (usually Hurlbut's *Story of the Bible*, easily understood by the younger children—I was number two of six), then we all went to our knees while Daddy prayed for each by name. We joined in the Lord's Prayer. Following supper in the evening, Daddy read a portion from Scripture and prayed again for all of us.

Our family was in a church one evening in Philadelphia when an invitation was given for those who wanted to take a stand for Christ. My brother Dave and I (he was ten, I was twelve) both stood up and verbally announced that we had received Christ as Savior. I wrote about it in the back of the Bible that my parents gave me in 1940.

Five of the six of us children became missionaries. The sixth was with InterVarsity for a time, then taught in a school for boys in England, and was a professor in several institutions in Massachusetts. At the funerals of our father and (years later) of our mother, we talked a great deal together about what we had learned from them, how they had visibly shown the love of Christ to us and to all who visited in our home. My mother kept a guest book which had forty-two countries represented in it. It was always a thrill to us children when foreign missionaries visited in our home. "We got used to the noise of suitcases bumping up and down the stairs," said our youngest brother one time. What a heritage we had. Thanks be to God!

Elisabeth Elliott's story of faith in Christ is remarkable. Do you have a faith that will carry you through life's extremities?

"You shall teach them diligently to your children, and shall talk of them when you sit in your house, when you walk by the way, when you lie down, and when you rise up" (Deut. 6:7 NKJV).

15

INCREDIBLE MESS TO INSPIRING MINISTRY

Ken Freeman

Environment and heredity have conspired to destroy many lives. Now you can read in Ken Freeman's own words how God snatched him out of the worst of circumstances to a fruitful life and ministry.

God can take a mess and make it a message. I've had nine step-fathers, twenty-four different schools, and slept in streets, garages, alleys, bars, cars, and in the backyard. My real dad walked out of my life when I was four years old. My mom became an alcoholic and started beating me and my sister. We lived with no love and in constant fear. I was molested at seven years old, and my sister was raped at five years old while my mom was out drinking and left us with her ex-boyfriend. I started drinking and smoking at nine and was put in jail at fifteen. My mom held a knife to my throat when

I was nine and convinced me I was a loser. I attempted suicide at nine. I didn't want to die; I wanted the pain to stop.

The sad part of my testimony is I didn't hear about God or Jesus until I was sixteen. My friend, Jeff, invited me to church in 1968 in Corpus Christi, Texas, and the first time I heard the gospel I got saved. My life has never been the same!

Now I've been married twenty-nine years, have two awesome sons, four grandkids, two beautiful daughters, and a great ministry. I've seen over two hundred thousand people come to Christ in the last seventeen years. I've written a book called *Rescued by the Cross*. I'm living proof that God can take a mess and make it a message. God has a plan and purpose (Jer. 29:11). I used to be an outcast, rebellious—the devil's brat. Praise God I'm now a King-kid, joint-heir, and saint. I've been adopted. Don't try God; trust Him!

As you have read Ken Freeman's testimony, you have read the miracle of God's grace. Doesn't Ken's experience destroy every excuse a person can give for not receiving Jesus? Will you let Jesus give you a new life?

"Come unto me, all ye that labour and are heavy laden, and I will give you rest. Take my yoke upon you, and learn of me; for I am meek and lowly in heart: and ye shall find rest unto your souls. For my yoke is easy, and my burden is light" (Matt. 11:28–30).

16

BOOKING ON CHRIST

Leonard G. Goss

Have you noticed that testimonies of true conversions are often strikingly similar, yet remarkably different? Some people remember most clearly their conviction of sin; others recall their specific moment of repentance and belief. Some can remember specific words in a sermon while others can recount the very words of repentance and faith that they voiced in prayer as they called on the Lord. Yet all of them speak of their belief in Jesus and the change of life that resulted. Len Goss recalls how God used his involvement in a high-school Bible club to bring him to the point when, at age sixteen, he joined his friends in their faith in Christ. He also remembers a time of surrender to the lordship of Christ and ultimately a call into Christian ministry. But let him share his pilgrimage in his own words.

My mother was Jewish and was raised in a devout Orthodox Jewish home in Brooklyn, New York. I always thought my father came from a background of no religion, at least that I ever knew of, but I found out after his death that he and his family (from Arkansas) came from the Baptist tradition. In any event, I was brought up without religious training or inclination of any kind.

During high school days I began attending Young Life meetings. Young Life was a rather popular club at my school, and it drew many students. I did not at that time know that Young Life International was a Christian ministry that actively sought to introduce high-school students to Jesus Christ. At first, I didn't think very much of the Christian talks, but I had a lot of fun singing, watching funny skits and stunts, being with friends, and so on.

I became very active in this club, and during my sophomore year I was asked to join "Campaigners," the Bible study group for the more serious Young Life kids. Our study text was the J. B. Phillips translation of the New Testament in modern English. When I began with Campaigners at the beginning of my sophomore year, the New Testament was a very foreign and curious thing indeed. Yet, by around the middle of that year, I realized with much amazement that I was reading the Bible as a new believer in Jesus Christ. What had happened was that I grew into an acceptance of Christianity. I continued to be extremely active in Young Life and Campaigners for the rest of high school, and I grew in Christ through that exposure.

I say I *grew* into an acceptance of Christianity, for it was a step in steps. My conversion was quite gradual. From a tradition of religious illiteracy, I took in more and more head knowledge about the Christian faith through Bible study and Christian fellowship. Soon, at sixteen, I joined my friends in belief. In my conversion experience the model was not a praying of a one-time prayer. Rather, it was a commitment to reading the gospel story, which led to reading the Bible through the eyes of faith—a demonstration of the power and importance of God's Word.

Still, at that point, I was not terribly interested in being identified with the Christian community. It was not until my college years, under the ministry of Campus Crusade for Christ, that I grew spiritually and dedicated my life to Christ's lordship.

At Arizona State University I became active in Campus Crusade, and in that way I continued my involvement in Christian ministry. The group was involved in Bible study, prayer, campus evangelism, and a large weekly evangelistic outreach called College Life—which I directed during my senior year. I was entrenched in all the aspects of campus ministry. On retreats, I helped in teaching seminars; on campus I was one of the leaders. This was the movement God seemed to be using on our campus, and I wanted to be a part of it. During these college years it soon became apparent to me that I was called to decide whether or not my life was going to be marked by the lordship of Christ. I chose to dedicate myself to the service of our Lord and His people, a decision I've never doubted or regretted, and an attitude I've not changed since that time. I have never failed to see that God has directed the circumstances of my life.

Two days after Carolyn graduated from ASU, we were married. A couple of months after this, we were in the Chicago area for seminary, where I took the pastoral program at Trinity Evangelical Divinity School (TEDS). During my third and fourth years at Trinity, I edited *Trinity Journal,* which was then a student-generated journal of scholarship. It was through this work and the influences of both Carl F. H. Henry and the late Paul E. Little that the Lord led me to pursue a career in literature evangelism and Christian publishing.

Though I pursued and completed the M.Div. degree at TEDS, and took additional graduate work in philosophy of religion elsewhere, for me the call to ministry was not to serve in the pastorate or on the mission field but rather to serve the church universal, and particularly the larger evangelical movement in this country, through the full-time ministry of Christian publishing. Christian writing and publishing are powerful and prominent tools for God's work in our world, and I am glad to play a small part in producing books to help readers be salt and light in society. In this capacity I have had over twenty years' experience working with Christian scholars, professors, pastors, and writers, developing books of excellence to serve Christians and to help them grow intellectually, emotionally, and spiritually in their quest to become what God intends.

Many people look back to a specific and memorable moment in time as the evidence of their conversion. But Jesus said that the ultimate evidence of real life is fruit—the outward expression of the inward nature. Is there fruit in your life, genuine evidence that Christ is alive in you, evidence that you have been born again from above?

"I am the vine, you are the branches. He who abides in Me, and I in him, bears much fruit; for without Me you can do nothing" (John 15:5 NKJV).

17

FAILURE LED TO VICTORY

Bill Gothard

At some point we all try to live a good life. But our best efforts fail us. In his own words, Bill Gothard confesses how as a ten-year-old boy his spiritual failure combined with the simple presentation of the gospel in a child evangelism class led him to Jesus. His initial desire to tell others about Jesus has borne abundant fruit in the special gift for spiritual music ministry that God gave him.

The idea startled me! It came to my mind one morning when I was about ten years old: *Why not go through this whole day without doing or saying anything wrong?* It seemed like an easy goal to achieve, so I set out to do it. However, even before the day ended, I realized how much I had failed. I took heart in the thought that I would try again the next day. After several days of failure, the awful realization came to me: *If God put all my good days on one side of His scale and my bad days on the other side, how would I ever get to heaven?*

That awareness of my sinful condition prepared me for what I heard several days later at a child evangelism class near our home. At the meeting, I heard for the first time that I was destined for eternal judgement but that Christ had died to pay the penalty for my sin. That evening I knelt in my bedroom and called upon the Lord for His salvation.

The next morning I had a new desire to read the Bible. I also wanted to tell all my friends about the salvation I had found. This became the goal and joy of my life.

———————

Little did Bill Gothard know just how God would use him to touch the lives of vast multitudes, calling them to faith in Christ and effective living. What potential is locked in your life just waiting for you to insert the key of faith?

"Except your righteousness shall exceed the righteousness of the scribes and Pharisees, ye shall in no case enter into the kingdom of heaven" (Matt. 5:20).

18

THE MIRACLE OF REAPING

Michael Gott

When you read the testimony of Natasha Matskevich, you will, no doubt, be interested to know more about the American preacher whom God used to reap such precious fruit in such a far-off and unlikely place. The preacher's name is Michael Gott. Isn't it a blessing that he has shared fully with us the story of his life-changing experience with the Lord Jesus? Now everyone can read his testimony.

With the passing of time I find myself rethinking the supernatural elements of my conversion, knowing it happened to me and yet looking at it with the almost-objective eyes of one who observed it happen to someone else.

I am awed by how the Holy Spirit quietly but purposefully prepared my heart to recognize my need for a Savior and Lord.

62

I now recognize that God used my sense of feeling empty within, my awareness of guilt, and my searching for something or someone worthy to be followed to awaken me spiritually. Someone in the 1800s once wrote these words so true of me: "He moved my soul to seek Him, seeking me!" That's it—perfectly capturing the behind-the-scenes process going on in my life.

The Sunday night of my conversion there was a very real sense of being irresistibly drawn to an encounter with Christ. For example, as a teenage boy of sixteen who had seldom attended church, I went to a church on a Sunday night alone. The sermon was not powerful or even fully evangelistic, but I was drawn to Christ. The preacher was a pastor preaching on an ordinary Sunday night. In fact, the subject of giving to God was emphasized as much as coming to Christ.

The significant point is that it was not the powerful sermon or the dynamic preacher or any other externals that I was conscious of but rather being inwardly attracted to a person—Jesus.

Possibly it is this realization that has caused me to have a lifetime of almost no doubts about my conversion. I have to stand back and say it cannot be explained in any other way but as the work of a loving God drawing me to Jesus. Today I am thankful I am not the product of a preacher with great personal charisma and personality who by that sheer power could induce people to respond.

I am very thankful now that the invitation was without coercion or manipulation. The urgency I felt was totally the work of the Holy Spirit. Today I recognize that my conversion was the result of the power of the Scripture and the ministry of God's

Spirit working in and through a rather ordinary message by a man who was not necessarily a great or gifted preacher.

So my conversion experience was without emotional embellishment; it was a real and quiet surrender. I was more aware, it now seems to me, that I was coming to a Lord than a Savior. A Savior, yes, but it was not a sense of impending judgment that was foremost in my mind but thoughts of yielding my life to one with a plan, with an agenda for my life, and He asked me to come to Him in full and unconditional surrender.

God is sovereign, and we cannot dictate to Him thoughts or stages through which He may choose to bring an individual to saving faith. I now believe my conversion had to do more with the simple witness of untrained witnesses and prayer on the part of those who somehow observed my spiritual needs. God chose, in His sovereignty, to work in that way in my life. How wonderful to be able to see that and to have an unshakable assurance that all of this is authentic.

And I walked away from my conversion experience without even the vocabulary to explain it adequately to my parents. They heard me stumble through a brief but sincere confession when I returned home. I received a sincere, two-word acknowledgment from my mother—"that's good"—and nothing more. But because it was so real, I did not need more. I went to sleep thanking God that I was now His. Years later I ran across words that captured my heart-thoughts as I awoke on that first Monday morning after being born again:

Heaven above a softer blue,
Earth around a sweeter green;
Something lives in very hue
Christless eyes have never seen.
O, this full and perfect peace!
O, what companionship I find
In His love which cannot cease
I am His, and He is mine.
—George Wade Robinson, 1838–77

No one discipled me personally, but within days I found a Bible, and I was reading the New Testament like a starving man at a banquet feast. I checked out of the local church library a single volume commentary and was soon researching Scripture on my own.

I still find it amazing—a teenage boy of almost seventeen totally transformed in a matter of hours. As I reflect on my conversion, I believe more strongly than ever that the Holy Spirit is the great communicator. It seems to me without His supernatural work there would be no such thing as conversion. He breaks down barriers and convicts of sin and brings home to the heart the truth of the gospel. True conversions and changed lives are in His hands. He quickened my heart, and to this day it is a glorious mystery.

Every Sunday morning and night I was at Sunday school and church. Sunday afternoons were spent beside the radio listening to sermons from H. H. Hobbs, Billy Graham, and C. M. Ward. It's interesting, I think, that all three were regularly preaching evangelistic sermons.

In those early waking days almost immediately there was a desire to walk with the Lord moment by moment and to openly confess Him before people; that was implanted into my heart.

Within weeks of my conversion, I recall being inclined to notice how preachers preached. I studied, unaware what it all meant then, their conclusions and persuasion and yet even then reacted to dubious means of getting a public response such as threats and pressure. In my youthful naivety I could not have possibly orchestrated such an unusual interest; that too was very much of God.

It was all part of being eventually called and shaped to spend my life as an evangelist of Jesus Christ. Even then I was being set apart for the work of an evangelist to devote my time and effort to this God-given task. It was, as I now forcefully acknowledge, the clear leading of God. It was and is a miracle of grace.

One of the discoveries of born-again people is that God has a remarkable and fulfilling purpose for their life—including the possibility of ministering to other cultures. Are you fulfilling God's purpose for your life?

"And I, if I be lifted up from the earth,
will draw all men unto me" (John 12:32).

19

Too Smart to Be Saved?

Charles Hand

Some people think that a genuine Christian conversion is only for those who are fearful and weak-minded. Charles Hand discovered that no one is so genuinely intelligent as when he trusts in Christ.

The Lord saved me when I was a few days short of my twenty-ninth birthday. I had been to the university, had a decent GPA, was accepted into Phi Theta Kappa, and had passed all the preliminaries to becoming part of Mensa but still could not understand what it meant to give your heart to Jesus. I was a businessman in west Texas, and Katie, my wife, attended a church almost across the street from where we lived. The preacher of that church came to talk to me. He was a good man, but I did not understand what he was saying. I remember telling him that if I could reach down into my chest and tear my heart out and hand it to Jesus, full well knowing that I would die doing it, I could do it!

I had almost come to the point of believing there was no such thing as being saved, for someone would speak to me about being saved and would say I should have faith. I would ask them to tell me what was faith. OK! Then how do I believe, and the answer was to have faith. It was a theological merry-go-round.

In my mind I compared it to having dinner at a person's home where the meal was a casserole. If I asked the hostess if she had prepared it and she said that she had, then if I asked for the recipe and she stuttered and stammered and gave me clichés, I would finally decide that she had not really cooked the casserole.

In one of the five or six times in our marriage of the same number of years, I took Katie to church at Miller Road Baptist Church in Garland, Texas. The following week the pastor, Jack Hyles, came to visit me. Sitting in my living room, he showed me the Roman Road. It was as if a light came on. Salvation was not just believing *in* Jesus but was believing *Jesus*. He promised He would save me if I would let Him! The only thing I had to decide was if He meant it.

The preacher asked me to kneel with him, but Katie was in the room. I could just see God calling down from heaven saying this was for people who hadn't done some of the things that I had done, then Katie would know how really wicked I had been. As soon as the preacher left, I went to bed. There in the blackness of the room, I told the Lord that if I were in His position I would not forgive and save someone such as I, but that man had showed me in the Book that Jesus had promised. I took Him at His word.

I remember saying, "You can take my life and do whatever you want. You sure couldn't do any worse than I have." I didn't hear the flutter of angels' wings, nor did I hear the angelic choir, but my first thought was, *Charley, why didn't you do that a long time ago?* My second thought was that had there been a Christian there I would have punched him out because he had made getting saved so complicated. My next thought was that I had wasted half a good life and should waste no more. I have wasted life since then but not nearly as much as before.

Since that day, April 21, 1955, I have tried to tell those who would listen and those who wouldn't that Jesus has promised to save them. Do they think He would lie to them?

———————

Pride can keep us from doing a lot of things, even the most important of all: trusting in Jesus as Savior. Are you willing to humble yourself and take God at His Word?

> *"Jesus said to him, 'If you can believe, all things are possible to him who believes'"* (Mark 9:23 NKJV).

20

WINNING THE WAR WITHIN

Stan Hannan

Often it is difficult to concentrate on the tragic circumstances occurring around the world because we are fighting our own wars within. Such was the case of Stan Hannan, a native of central Africa, who was serving his time in the military forces during a fierce civil war.

Born and raised in central Africa, I was required to serve a period in the military. While serving in the forces, I met Norma, a teacher in a local school in a small town on the edge of the Zambezi valley. This was in 1966 and the start of the civil war in Zimbabwe. In reality, Norma was the first "born-again" Christian I had encountered. Not only did I perceive her as beautiful to look at; there was a quality and integrity about her that was compelling. Coming from a non-Christian home, and having had no involvement with the Bible or church, I found myself intrigued by her dignity, honesty, and obedience to her faith. She clearly followed Jesus and had no hesitation to share her commitment with me.

My life was in shambles, the smell of death was around me constantly, and I had watched friends die. While I held to a vague and expansive faith in God, I had no idea what a true Christian was or should be—that is, until I fell in love with and married Norma in August of 1967. We married with a cloud of uncertainty hanging over our future because of the strife and political climate of southern Africa. My own personal life had disintegrated into heavy drinking, socializing, and generally poor behavior. Norma was disappointed in me but remained faithful, loving, and supportive.

After leaving the military, I went into business and traveled the world, generally without Norma. We grew apart, but she hung on to our relationship with a tenacity that amazed me. She wanted children and a home. I wanted fame, fortune, and freedom from responsibility.

On a rainy day in 1973, at a time when I felt our marriage was falling apart, I went one more time with her to church. I had most times rejected her invitation. Church bored me, and I was mystified that people found church an important part of their lives. But on this day somehow the Holy Spirit broke through to my soul. At the invitation I went forward and said to the preacher, as I turned and pointed to my wife, "I want what she has." I then fell on my knees and asked Jesus Christ to forgive me, allow me to change my ways, and to come into my heart. I was twenty-eight years of age. I then took her into my arms and said, "Can we start again?" We had been married for six years at this time.

God broke loose in our lives. Norma became pregnant with our first child, a daughter called Deborah. Two more daughters, Barbara and Kerri-Anne, were to follow in the next years. In an amazing "Damascus Road" experience, God called me to the ministry and I obeyed. I was ordained into the ministry and as an army chaplain three years later.

We have ministered together for the past twenty-five years as I traveled the world as an evangelist and served God as an army chaplain. The Lord allowed us to immigrate to America in 1985. After a two-year period of traveling across this beautiful land to speak in churches, we have for the past fourteen years served as pastor to the First Baptist Church of Eustis in Florida.

After these years I could fill pages with stories of God and His faithfulness, but in the still hours of the early morning, I reflect on what he has done. Norma and I have recently celebrated our thirty-third anniversary, and I love her more than ever. I remember leading my mother and father to Christ, baptizing my brother, baptizing all three of my daughters, conducting their weddings, watching our grandchildren sing and smile in church, helping many close friends to accept the claims of Jesus, being part of God's work around the world, becoming citizens of America, and watching hundreds baptized in the church we serve!

God's mercy, majesty, forgiveness, tolerance, and love are beyond comprehension. His Word abides forever! "If anyone is in Christ he is a new creation, old things have passed away, behold all things become new" (2 Cor. 5:17).

———

Stan Hannan's testimony is an encouragement to anyone who wishes for the internal war of the soul to cease and the peace of God to reign. Have you found that peace with God?

"He brought me up also out of an horrible pit, out of the miry clay, and set my feet upon a rock, and established my goings. And he hath put a new song in my mouth, even praise unto our God" (Ps. 40:2–3).

21

RESPONDING THE FIRST TIME

O. S. Hawkins

There are many accounts of people who came to God only after many appeals by many people over many years. Such was not the case with O. S. Hawkins. He writes of responding the very first time he heard the Good News.

I came to know Christ as a seventeen-year-old high school senior in Fort Worth, Texas. Even though I grew up in what many refer to as the "Buckle of the Bible Belt," I was basically biblically illiterate, not even knowing that Matthew, Mark, Luke, and John were books of the Bible. After a basketball game one evening, I was walking to my car in the parking lot when a young man I had previously known from a different high school in Fort Worth approached me. He and I were friends there in our sophomore and junior years, but

I had not seen him in about a year. He began to tell me how Christ had come into his life and what a transformation it had made.

Initially, I thought he was crazy, but I could not get away from what he said. The next Sunday morning he came by my home and took me to Sagamore Hill Baptist Church in Fort Worth, where I heard Fred Swank preach the gospel. It was the first time I remember hearing this Good News, and I received Christ as my Savior on that Sunday morning, January 3, 1965. Although I'm not what I ought to be today, I've never been the same since that day.

God's Word says, "Seek the Lord while He may be found; call upon Him while He is near" (Isa. 55:6). That's more than just good advice. It is a reminder that we must come when He calls and on His terms—or we don't come at all.

"He first findeth his own brother Simon, and saith unto him, We have found the Messias, which is, being interpreted, the Christ. And he brought him to Jesus" (John 1:41–42a).

22

JUST KEN AND HIS DAD

Ken Hemphill

The service was over. The people were gone. The preacher was now just Dad. Read about this wonderful memory!

———————————

I had the joy and privilege of being raised in a Christian home. My dad was a Baptist preacher from the foothills of North Carolina. My parents taught me about God's love through word and deed from the day of my birth. My love for Christ and His church was nurtured by my entire family. When I was nine years old, I became sensitized to my own sin. Dad's sermons seemed to be directed at me when he talked of the consequences of sin and the need for forgiveness.

One Sunday night after church, I followed Dad to the vestibule of the church. After everyone left, I told him that I wanted to invite

76

Jesus to come into my heart and to be my Savior. That night in the vestibule of a little country church, my dad told me how I could turn from my sin and turn to Jesus. With the songwriter, I can say, "Every day with Jesus is sweeter than the day before."

———————

There is no greater joy for a parent than leading a child to faith in Christ. No greater privilege! No greater responsibility!

"And the things that thou hast heard of me among many witnesses, the same commit thou to faithful men, who shall be able to teach others also" (2 Tim. 2:2).

23

THE IMPACT OF OUR HERITAGE

Jim Henry

Many people are left with a heritage that must be overcome in order to turn to God. Others, however, are blessed to discover that this heritage is a constant reminder of the grace of God. Jim Henry writes of being a fourth-generation believer.

The genesis of my personal relationship with our Lord Jesus Christ began with the foundation of a godly great-grandmother, grandmother, and mother. They got me in the Bible and in the church from the earliest days I can remember. My mother told me in later years that she had dedicated me to the Lord and His service at a women's Bible study when she was pregnant with me.

I came to a sense of conviction and lostness during an old-fashioned tent revival. Some time later, on a hot August morning in a rural church near Springfield, Tennessee, I stepped forward making my public decision to accept Jesus as my Savior. I followed in baptism several months later at the First Baptist Church of Nashville.

Shortly after I began my ministry, I experienced a season of doubt. I began to examine myself as Paul urged in 2 Corinthians 13:5. I looked to see if my walk matched my profession. One morning in my study, the Holy Spirit manifested Himself in my heart in a profound way, assuring me of His love and my position in Him. My constant assurance is looking at Jesus' finished work on the cross and His Word: "These things are written that you may know that you have eternal life and who believe in the name of the Son of God" (1 John 5:13). I count myself blessed that Jesus would save me and call me as His undershepherd. For more than fifty-five years, I have known Him. For more than forty years I've been His servant, and the longer I know Him, the sweeter He grows.

Is there someone in your past who has directed your attention toward God? Will there be those in the future who will thank God because of the influence of your life on their faith?

"When I call to remembrance the genuine faith that is in you, which dwelt first in your grandmother Lois and your mother Eunice, and I am persuaded [it dwells] in you also"
(2 Tim. 1:5 NKJV).

24

AROUND THE WORLD FROM A TWO-ROOM HOME

Rudy Hernandez

"Mighty oaks from little acorns grow." But it takes a remarkable work of God to make it happen. Rudy Hernandez experienced such a work of God. You will be amazed that from a two-room house, God has taken him around the world . . . literally.

Bullets from the pistol of a godfather took my dad's life when I was only ten months old. My mother moved my six sisters and me to the small two-room house my dad had built for us in San Antonio, Texas. She was a good mom but had nothing more than her goodness to offer. She did not know God, though when I was two and at the point of death, she had sought Him by saying,

"Whoever You are, wherever You are, I plead with You, save my son from death, and You can do whatever You want with him." A friend of the family took us to Dr. E. Y. Somma, who said, "If he takes the hourly dose of this medication through six in the morning, he may make it." I took the final dose. God spared my life.

Eight years later my sister Ramona had committed to attend a meeting at the Rosillo Street Baptist Mission in west San Antonio. Due to a school schedule, she was unable to keep her commitment. My mom, a firm believer that "a king's word is never retracted," reprimanded her, and Mom and I went in her place. I went to church by mistake—a mistake that launched me on the greatest journey of my life.

My mother and I attended and enjoyed what we heard and saw. We returned numerous times until on May 26, 1938, as a ten-year-old shoeshine boy, I was sitting on the roughly made pew in the one-car garage converted into a chapel when I felt God speaking to me. "Jesus loves you, He died for you, take Him into your heart." My heart was breaking. In tears and barefooted, I almost ran, gave my hand to pastor Paul Mason and, repentant of my sins, asked the Lord Jesus Christ into my life. Joy was heaped upon joy as Mom followed me down the aisle. She too was asking Christ into her life.

I spotted a blind man, Mr. Martinez, uneasy as if needing to do likewise. I went to him and asked him if he also wanted to trust Jesus as his Savior. He replied, "If you will take me." Since I had led him by the hand from one place to another, I knew what to do. I literally led him to Christ.

At thirteen, three years later, my mother heard me preach my first sermon. She got me aside and told me of her having given me to God if He would spare me from death. She said, "Now I know what happened eleven years ago, and my commitment has just been rewarded."

Having circumnavigated the globe, everywhere in the more than sixty countries I have touched in my ministry of more than half a century, my mother and brother Paul have been there with me. One is because of a commitment made and the other because of a calling obeyed. To God be the glory!

Many people consistently excuse their bad behavior by blaming tragic circumstances early in life. But when you meet Jesus, all your excuses melt away. After all, you won't need them anymore.

"For this child I prayed; and the LORD *hath given me my petition which I asked of him: Therefore also I have lent him to the* LORD; *as long as he liveth he shall be lent to the* LORD*"*
(1 Sam. 1:27–28).

25

RELIGIOUS BUT LOST
Ron Herrod

Billy Graham has said that a large percentage of Christian church members have stopped short of a saving relationship with the Christ they profess to worship. This was true of Ron Herrod. He had the profession but lacked the reality. Read in his own words Ron's experience and the reasons for the spiritual failure.

Many times people will tell me, "I think I am saved." Others will say, "I guess I am saved." Still others will respond by saying, "I don't believe you can ever really know." I am thrilled to say, "I know I am saved because I was there when it happened."

I was brought up in a Christian home. For that I will be eternally grateful. Every young person with Christian parents should never cease to praise the Lord. My mom and dad brought me up to go to church regularly.

At a very young age, I saw my friends joining the church and felt like it was something I would like to do. So after talking to the pastor, I made my profession of faith and was baptized. Joining the church did not change my life at all. I continued to grow up being religious but lost.

When I was fifteen, my mother made me go to Vacation Bible School in our church. Thank God for parents who insist that their children go to church. That is one of the finest things you will ever do for your children. I resented my mother making me go, but it was one of the greatest things she ever did for me. At Vacation Bible School, I heard about a youth camp and I decided to go.

When we arrived at Camp Lake Forest in Macon, Mississippi, on July 5, 1958, I immediately noticed that there was something different about this place. People were actually talking about Jesus Christ and having a great time. Everything was exciting and different but always Christ-centered.

At the party that night, a former Hollywood movie star by the name of Redd Harper played guitar and sang about Jesus Christ. He had starred in several Billy Graham films. By the end of this so-called "party," I was pretty disgusted with all this religion stuff and went to my cabin to get a good night's sleep.

As I was dozing off to sleep, an energetic young counselor bounced into the room and announced it was time for the devotion. *Oh, no,* I thought, *more church.* That night Jim Barron read to us from the third chapter of the Gospel of John. For the first time in my life, I saw myself as a lost sinner in need of a Savior.

Jim read to us about a man named Nicodemus (John 3:1–21). I learned several things that night about Nicodemus that I have never forgotten. I immediately saw myself in the shoes of this character from the pages of the Bible. Perhaps knowing some things about this man will also help you to know things about yourself.

Nicodemus was a religious man. The Bible tells us he was a Pharisee, which was the highest religious order of his day. In addition to that, he was a ruler of the Jews. So Nicodemus was a highly religious, sincere, moral man. Many people believe that by simply being sincere they will be saved. The truth is there are many sincere people in hell. It is possible to be sincerely wrong. Nicodemus is living proof that a moral life may keep you out of jail, but it won't keep you out of hell. Even though he had the finest kind of human robes in righteousness, they were as filthy rags. He needed the righteous robes that only Christ can give.

Nicodemus had a head knowledge of Christ. In John 3:2, Nicodemus revealed that he knew all about Jesus Christ. It is possible to know all about a person and not really know him. Many know about the President of the United States, but they do not really know him. Nicodemus needed a two-foot conversion "from his head to his heart." Salvation does involve an intellectual acceptance of the historical fact of Christ. It does involve an emotional commitment to Jesus Christ, but it also involves a volitional commitment of your life to Jesus Christ. By that, I mean a commitment of your will to His will.

Nicodemus was spiritually blind. Jesus told him that unless he was born again, he could not see the kingdom of God. This did not mean that Nicodemus would not some day see heaven, but it meant that Nicodemus could not then and there understand the things of God. The natural man cannot comprehend spiritual things.

Nicodemus had a questioning spirit. Naturally, Nicodemus was puzzled about this strange thing Jesus talked about. What was the new birth? Could a man enter into his mother's womb and be born again? But Jesus had all the right answers and shared with Nicodemus that if he would turn from his sin and believe on the Lord Jesus Christ, he would be saved.

That night, under Jim Barron's leadership, I did exactly what the Bible says to do. I learned the necessity of repentance for the first time. You can go to heaven without ritual or religion—but not without repentance. I turned from my sin and invited Jesus Christ to become the Lord of my life. I know I was saved. I was there when it happened.

What would be the result if you made an honest evaluation of your spiritual state on the basis of Bible standards?

"Unless you repent you will all likewise perish"
(Luke 13:3 NKJV).

26

NO ONE HAD WITNESSED, AND THEN . . .

Junior Hill

For a thirteen-year-old boy to have lived in the United States and never to have entered a church seems impossible! But that was Junior Hill's experience. Now read in his own words how a Gideon New Testament, a concerned invitation to attend Sunday school, and the impact of gospel preaching was used by the Holy Spirit to lead a boy to Jesus as Savior.

Although my parents were decent and hardworking people who loved and provided for me as best they could, I was reared in a home where family members never went to church. Religion was simply not a part of our activities. I was almost thirteen years old before I ever entered the door of any church. To my knowledge, no one ever witnessed to me or shared the Good News of how to be saved. For all practical purposes, I was a pagan—uninformed, unaware, and uninterested in a part of life that meant nothing to me.

The closest I ever came to hearing about God and His grace was the day the local Gideons came to our school and gave all the students a red New Testament. Although I didn't know what it was all about, I treasured that little book, for I was told it was a book about God. When I was thirteen years old, Mrs. Zula Montgomery, a faithful member of the First Baptist Church, Hartselle, Alabama, invited me to come to Sunday school. I had no idea what it was all about. But at her insistence and the encouragement of some of my friends, I went to church for the first time. Because of the love and concern of my teachers and fellow classmates, I was soon attending regularly—not only Sunday school but Training Union as well.

As I sat in those classes, the Lord was slowly but surely preparing my heart for salvation. Four years later, as a seventeen-year-old boy, I received Christ as my Savior and was baptized by my pastor, Dr. D. C. Stringfellow, in 1954.

Unlike many others, my experience was not dramatic or earthshaking. I was not overcome with great emotions and fanfare. I have often wished that I was. But as best I knew, with my limited background, I gave my life to Christ that day. The *beginning* might not have been so glamorous, but the *continuing* has been wonderful! For almost fifty years I have loved and served Him. He has blessed and honored me in ways I could never fathom. With all my heart I am glad to confess to all the world that Jesus Christ is my Savior, my Lord, and my Master.

———————

Junior Hill now regularly invites others into this same relationship. Will you accept his invitation? The result is wonderful!

"For the word of God is quick, and powerful, and sharper than any twoedged sword" (Heb. 4:12).

27

FROM POOLROOM TO PULPIT

Johnny Hunt

Johnny Hunt, a powerful communicator, shares the true story of his incredible journey from the Sunset Park Poolroom to the pulpit of a great church.

———————

I grew up in Wilmington, North Carolina. I came from a broken home, and my mom had to work two jobs to take care of six children. I was a rebellious child. At the age of eleven, I experienced what it meant to be drunk. At the age of fourteen, I became a regular at Sunset Park Poolroom. At the age of sixteen, I got my driver's license. I was really a shy young man, and I just couldn't stand before a crowd of people and speak—so I quit school. It was nothing but downhill from there.

Then I met Janet and we fell immediately in love. Finally after a lengthy courtship (I think it was six whole months!), I asked her to be my wife. We were married on November 21, 1970. After a while Janet began encouraging me to go to church. I would do anything and everything I could to keep from going to church. In December of 1972, after attending Long Leaf Baptist Church for several weeks, God began to bring me under deep conviction. Everything would be fine as long as the sermon was being preached or somebody was singing. Then the preacher would say, "We're going to stand together in a moment and sing an invitation hymn." I don't know what would happen to me, but each time I would begin to weep. Someone told me—and now I understand after being a Christian—that I was experiencing conviction.

The afternoon of January 7, 1973, I sat nervously awaiting the evening service. I had never been to an evening service in my entire life. I had every reason in the world not to go to church. But in my heart of hearts, I really wanted to give my life to Jesus Christ. I wanted to invite Him into my heart and give Him an opportunity to change my life, if indeed, He was the one who could do it.

Usually we would walk in the church and sit near the back. But I knew I was going to be going forward that night, and I didn't want to walk a long way. So we moved up to the third pew from the front. I didn't want to have to climb over anybody. I wanted to make it as easy as possible!

I knew that when the invitation was given, I would be going forward to entrust my life to Jesus Christ. Earlier that afternoon I had prayed, "Dear Lord, I am going to come down tonight to trust You. I'd appreciate it if You'd help me not to cry." That night when the invitation was given, I didn't cry. I just went down, and

I told the preacher, "I want to give my heart and life to Jesus Christ." I'll never forget that moment; it's indelibly written in my heart and mind. That night, January 7, 1973, *Jesus changed my life!*

What I'm trying to communicate in this brief testimony is that, from the poolroom to the pulpit, what really happened to me is that *Jesus Christ changed my life.* It was a simple, childlike experience. I simply believed with all my heart that on the cross, two thousand years ago, Jesus really died. They took Him down from the cross, wrapped His body, and placed Him in a borrowed tomb. And for three days the Lord Jesus Christ was literally dead and buried. But on the third day, early in the morning, Jesus, the living Son of God, rose from the dead! He sent the Holy Spirit of God into this world to convict our hearts of our sin and our need for Him. And He sent the Word of God to show us the way to heaven when we die. So now it is my mission to tell everyone the message that what Jesus did for me He will do for you.

Every sermon I preach is integrated with the fact that *Jesus is in the life-changing business!*

Doesn't what Johnny Hunt shared make you dream about life's possibilities? Nothing is impossible with God.

"Therefore if any man be in Christ, he is a new creature: old things are passed away; behold, all things are become new"
(2 Cor. 5:17).

Testimony taken from Johnny M. Hunt, *Out of the Poolroom,* 1995.

28

JESUS IN
WASHINGTON, D.C.

Jim Inhofe

To most Americans, September 11 is Doomsday, but to one congressman, the Honorable Jim Inhofe, September 11, 1988, is the blessed day he met Jesus Christ in the members' dining room in the nation's capital. Now you can read what happened in his own words.

It is interesting that for many, many years before I was elected to the U.S. House of Representatives in 1986, I had thought of myself as being a born-again Christian. It wasn't until I got involved in the Christian Embassy in Washington that I realized I was in the same situation that many of the people in your congregation are in. I had never actually asked Jesus to come into my life as my personal Lord and Savior.

It finally happened at 2:30 on the afternoon of September 11, 1988, in the members' dining room in our nation's capital. It was called to my attention that my acceptance of Jesus had never taken place. So we bowed and prayed right there in the members' dining room, and Jesus came into my life. At that time I was involved in a lot of controversial things. This was one of those rare times when at the very moment that Jesus came into my life, all these changes took place in my life, and it has been great ever since.

I'm now involved in a mission in West Africa based on Acts 19:15 and Acts 2:42. I call it the "Political Strategy of Jesus." That is, His name—taking the name of Jesus to the kings mainly in West Africa. I have now been in eleven countries. Miracles have taken place, civil wars have stopped, and wonderful things have been going on.

There are a lot of people in the U.S. Senate and the House of Representatives who meet every week. In the case of the Senate, there is a prayer breakfast every Wednesday morning and Bible study with the chaplain of the Senate at noon every Thursday. An incredible number of people attend. People need to know that Jesus is alive and well in the nation's capital.

What a joy to read Inhofe's declaration: "Jesus is alive and well in the nation's capital." Is He alive and well in your heart?

"But as many as received him, to them gave he power to become the sons of God, even to them that believe on his name" (John 1:12).

29

FINDING LIFE AT THE BOTTOM OF THE BARREL

Joe Kalil

Inspiring books, friendly advice, and formal worship only increased Joe Kalil's frustration. What he really needed was a simple witness from an earnest believer. Joe's testimony reveals the importance of sticking to the facts. In his own words, he tells how God lifted a great weight from his shoulders.

I grew up knowing about God, even attended a religious elementary school. Most of my knowledge about God came from my grandmother, who prayed, it seemed, continuously. I also remember seeing my father on his knees praying every night, and to this day I believe he still does. Sadly, he never shared his faith with us.

I do not ever remember him saying what or to whom he was praying. I knew about Jesus; I knew about the crucifixion; I knew all the events that led to it. But I did not know why or for what purpose all of these things had happened.

Basically I knew about God but did not know God. In all my worshiping experiences at church and at school, the Bible was never introduced. The priest read passages that were in the Bible, but the congregation only got a printed booklet that guided you through the sermon and responses for that day.

As I became older, I found no satisfaction or fulfillment in the things I was exposed to. I needed to find my purpose in life. I needed to know why I was here. I began searching, always knowing in the back of my mind that there was only one true God, but not knowing how to get to Him. I searched, read (never the Bible), asked people for their opinions (what a mistake that was), and after several years came to the conclusion that I just had to make do with what I had.

So I started building my life as I knew best. My immediate family relations were not the best, and I looked elsewhere for the closeness of family. This whole period of searching and building a life on nothing (worldly views) took about eighteen years. Just when I thought everything seemed in order (I had a job, a wife, a home), it all came crashing down, and I found myself with more questions and a deeper hole in my soul than before.

As I returned to my search, I approached my priest to no avail. As I spoke to new acquaintances, several new options were given. One was a Christian counselor. At this point I was ready to try just about anything. I will never forget September 24, 1991, when this man of God took the time to share the gospel with me and explain what Jesus had done for me. I remember asking myself, *Why is this man telling me this story? I already know about God and Jesus. What I need is to fix my problem.* Little did I know that the root of my problem was not having a personal relationship with God. On this day I received Jesus in my heart, His forgiveness, and my first Bible. For the first time I felt fulfilled. A great weight was lifted off my shoulders. I started reading the Word and learning to give my life to God's will.

I cannot say that my life has been easy since then, but I am fulfilled. I still sin (truly try not to) but am forgiven. The closer I grow to God, the more joy and peace I feel. Circumstances and life bring difficulties, but nothing overshadows the peace and joy in my heart, knowing that He will always provide a way. I see life and my purpose in it in a new light. I thank God for Dr. Ted Place, who took the time to share with me the truth, the gospel of Jesus Christ. I no longer depend on me but on God's will for my life because His will is perfect. He has and will continue to prune and teach me, and I am so thankful that He loves me enough to do that.

Salvation depends not on what you know but on whom you know. Do you know Jesus?

"And this is life eternal, that they might know thee the only true God, and Jesus Christ, whom thou hast sent" (John 17:3).

30

AFFIRMATION . . . AND CONFIRMATION
Charles S. Kelley

Will God, the Creator and Sustainer of the universe, make a promise to a ten-year-old? Charles (Chuck) Kelley, president of one of the world's largest seminaries, would answer the questions with a resounding, "Yes!" Having "walked the aisle" as a young boy, he discovered that the Lord to whom he was committing himself would also make a commitment to him, a promise to bring him through to an unshakable confirmation of his salvation. Now read about two remarkable events in his life.

I had the joy of growing up in a wonderful Christian home. My mom and dad were committed Christians in a Christian marriage determined to raise children in a Christian home. From my earliest memories, I heard about Jesus at home and at church. We were deeply involved in every church activity, attended all church events, had visiting preachers in our home, and lived in an atmosphere in which absorbing knowledge of God was as natural as breathing. Bible reading, Scripture memory, and prayer were fixtures of life as a Kelley. I could not begin to count the number of times I heard the gospel shared, discussed, and explained at home and church. Before I was a teenager I could quote more Bible verses than many adults in the church.

When I was about ten years old, Dr. Wayne Ward, a family cousin and professor at Southern Seminary, came to my church to preach a revival. He preached wonderful sermons in the worship services and came to the house and told us wonderful stories of all sorts afterwards. On the last night of the revival meeting, I just knew it was time for me to do what I had seen so many people do over the brief years of my life. It was my time to walk the aisle and give my life to Jesus, and be baptized as a Christian.

God was so gracious to me as I grew. We had wonderful music and youth programs that made church a magnetic attraction for me and my friends. Great adults taught me in Sunday school and Discipleship Training. Our family life was a joy. By God's grace there was no time of rebellion, no resistance to continuing in the faith, no veering away from immersion in the life and world of following Jesus. A child's faith became a youth's desire to live for God and God alone. Yet still God had for me one further encounter that forever confirmed my life and identity in Christ.

We were traveling back from a family vacation along the Minnesota-Canada border. We spent the night before our journey home in a Holiday Inn in Duluth, Minnesota. I was preparing to begin my junior year in high school. As a special treat that night, I had a room all to myself. I had no problems bothering me, no crises creating anxiety. As I lay in bed that night, however, I began to think about my relationship with God. I thought of all the time I had spent in church. I thought of all the Bible verses I could quote. I thought of my squeaky clean lifestyle and wondered what all of that meant to God.

Suddenly I realized that only one thing would ever matter to God: Was I willing to trust Him completely with my life? All the things I might not have understood at ten were now completely clear. Jesus and Jesus alone had the power to save and keep me. My life and my habits would never be enough. The Christ I confessed as a child was alone responsible for my salvation. Some time during that night I slipped out of bed and got on my knees. I prayed a very simple prayer, affirming afresh my complete trust and complete commitment to Him.

A child's faith and a youth's desire for a Christian life matured into an overwhelming sense of gratitude for God's grace and a commitment to live for His glory for the rest of my life. Faith, understanding, and gratitude: I can never think of my salvation without reliving God's wonderful gifts!

A man once said that as a young boy he committed to Christ all of himself he knew to commit. "Then," he said, "I discovered that

Christ committed Himself to bringing me through to a complete understanding of His grace." Have you trusted completely in Christ and, like Chuck Kelley, come through to the point of full assurance?

"These things have I written unto you that believe on the name of the Son of God; that ye may know that ye have eternal life" (1 John 5:13).

31

THE UNLIKELY SERMON

Rick Kunz

A teenager, Justin, had gone to hear evangelist Billy Graham preach. Though Justin was not a Christian, he repeated what he had heard to his friend, Rick. Now you can read in Rick Kunz's own words how this unlikely sermon eventually led him and later his friend, Justin, to a life-changing experience with Jesus Christ. In fact, it led to Rick's becoming a career missionary.

I had just fallen asleep on the first night of a weeklong summer camp in central Florida when my best friend and fellow Boy Scout, Justin, roused me from my sleeping bag. I found out later that he had just arrived at camp after attending a Billy Graham Crusade in Jacksonville. Some classmates had dared Justin to attend, saying that if he did he would be saved. He wasn't. All Justin told me then was that he had something to tell me.

We went alone into a dining hut about one o'clock in the morning. I sat on a bench while he stood preaching the message he had just heard. I should add that Justin had a phenomenal memory and was a gifted communicator, able to share word for word, including Bible verses and references, what he had just heard.

When he finished sharing the invitation to receive Christ, I remember thinking two things—how simple the gospel message was and why hadn't someone shared this with me before. After all, I was already fifteen years old!

I didn't say yes to Jesus that night, but about two months later I was home alone with a Bible verse bouncing around in my head. I knew I was a sinner in need of a Savior. I knew Jesus was the promised Messiah and that I needed to accept Him. I phoned Justin just to make sure I remembered correctly what I needed to do to become a Christian. After I hung up, I went to my bedroom and knelt by my bed and prayed. I acknowledged Jesus as Lord and Savior, asking Him to forgive me and enter my life. I became a Christian that day. Shortly after, so did Justin.

———

Rick's testimony is evidence that God will go to surprising lengths to ensure that you hear the gospel. In fact, you have heard it already. How have you responded?

"For the preaching of the cross is to them that perish foolishness; but unto us which are saved it is the power of God" (1 Cor. 1:18).

32

FROM BOY-THIEF TO THEOLOGIAN

Richard Land

Conviction over the theft of a Ted Williams baseball bat laid the spiritual foundation for a leader who has been elected to represent the moral standards of a great association of churches to our national government. Richard Land tells the story of his confession that led to a life-changing experience.

I was converted to faith in Jesus Christ at an early age. I can never remember a time when I did not know through the teaching of my Christian mother that Jesus loved me, Jesus died for me, and Jesus had a wonderful plan that was tailor-made just for my life. I was at church virtually every time the church doors were open—Sunday morning, Sunday night, Wednesday night—and I took part in all of the children's choirs and the

Wednesday night ministry programs for children in Southern Baptist life.

Just before I turned six years old, I became personally convicted that I was a sinner and that I did things that were wrong, I said things that were wrong, I thought things that were wrong, and I knew that those actions and words and thoughts had made it necessary for Jesus to die on the cross. I had a tremendous sense of conviction about that time. It came to a head when my best friend who lived next door moved away, and I noticed that his Ted Williams baseball bat was still on the carport. He and his family had left, the movers hadn't moved it yet, and I thought, *I could take that bat, and he would think it was lost in the moving. He would be in another state, and he would never see the bat again. I could have that Ted Williams baseball bat, which is a lot better than my bat.*

So I stole that bat and put it under my bed and thought that I would feel really good. But instead, I had a tremendous sense of conviction and guilt. As I lay in bed that night, I imagined I could feel the glow from the heat of that baseball bat on my conscience as it lay under my bed. Finally, the only thing to do was to get up, get the bat from under the bed, and to take it out to my parents and explain to them what I had done. Through the process of confessing to them, I confessed my sins to Jesus and asked the Lord to come into my heart and save me. And He did. Then, of course, I made restitution to my friend whom I had wronged.

I must say that I didn't understand everything. I still don't understand everything. But I knew enough, and I understood enough to know that I was a sinner, that the wages of sin is death, and that Jesus died on the cross for my sins. If I trusted Him as Savior and Lord and accepted the price that He paid, He would come in and live in my heart forever. That was forty-six years ago. There have been too many times that I have not been everything that He would have me to be. But there has never been one single moment during that entire time when He has not been everything He said He would be to me and more.

If you miss a plane, it makes no difference whether you miss it by a minute or by an hour. Similarly, regardless of how "little" you think your sin might be, it has separated you from God. Repentance of sin and faith in Christ is the answer!

"He who covers his sins will not prosper, but whoever confesses and forsakes them will have mercy" (Prov. 28:13 NKJV).

33

HELLFIRE!
Tim Lee

Tim Lee is a highly decorated Marine who lost both legs during enemy action in Vietnam. Yet it was a sermon on the fire of hell that turned his heart to God. Now he has an evangelistic ministry that spans the globe.

I was raised in a Baptist preacher's home. Mom and Dad both lived godly lives. They lived what they preached.

I was ten years old, sitting on the second row on Sunday morning at the Norris City Baptist Church, Norris City, Illinois. As Dad preached that morning, I became miserable. All I could see was hell. I know that's not the only reason to be saved. But it is not a bad reason for getting saved.

At the time of the invitation, I went forward and Mom and

Dad came to pray and talk with me. I received Christ as my Savior and was born into the family of God.

Isn't it interesting how God gives us the opportunity to prepare for the unseen battles yet to come? Have you prepared for whatever may come by trusting in Jesus?

> *"I can do all things through Christ who strengthens me"*
> *(Phil. 4:13 NKJV).*

34

FROM COMMUNISM TO CHRIST

Natasha Matskevich

Although Natasha Matskevich spoke Russian, she was studying English. To improve her English, she went to a meeting to hear the American, Michael Gott, preach. Now Natasha tells how what she heard became a life-changing experience.

My name is Natasha Matskevich, and I am from the Belarussian town of Zhabinka. My native tongue is Russian. I was reared in a typical home for my country. I live in a small apartment with my good, hardworking parents, but they are without any living faith in Christ. My father works at an asphalt plant and my mother at the post office. (My father makes less than $600 per year.) My brother and I grew up in a strongly communist world near the city of Brest. As long as I can remember, Lenin's statue dominated our city square. We lived only a few miles away from the busy major motorway that crosses Europe to Moscow.

My town had no Baptist witness at all until about five years ago, and then a Baptist church started in Zhabinka. One day I heard an American was going to speak at the Baptist church. Because I was learning English in my school, I wanted to hear him, so I went. But within a few moments after he stood to speak, I was not thinking of learning English but thinking of my own spiritual needs. Michael Gott was boldly preaching Christ, and I was listening with all my heart as he repeated the words, "Will you invite Christ to live in your life?"

When Michael finished his message, I was so moved by the Holy Spirit and so powerfully drawn to Christ that I was unable to resist the call to come to Him. I knelt and repented and prayed at the front of the church with others. Something wonderful happened in my life. Jesus became real to me, and now He was living in my heart.

At first my parents thought I was in some strange religious sect, and they were very afraid and concerned, but they saw something real. Three years ago I was baptized as a Baptist believer in a river near my town. Many who were not believers came to watch; however, my father did not come. But later I was surprised to learn that my parents even told some of their friends, "We have a real Christian in our family!"

Now I only want to follow Christ in my life. Jan and Michael have made it possible for me to study in a Baptist college in America. So I am one of those people—and there are hundreds more—who come to Christ every year because of the clear, Christ-centered preaching of Michael Gott. Now my life is being blessed by the love of Jan and Michael. They are like spiritual parents to me. All glory to God, now and forever.

———————————

You surely noticed that Natasha's life-changing experience brought joy and peace. Have you discovered such joy and peace?

"Howbeit when he, the Spirit of truth, is come, he will guide you into all truth: for he shall not speak of himself; but whatsoever he shall hear, that shall he speak" (John 16:13).

35

JOSH CONFRONTS

Josh McDowell

Josh is a fighter. Early life made him angry but determined to succeed. He confronted Christians with skepticism, confronted Christ with determination to unmask. Now you can read the story of Josh's life-changing experience in his own words.

I arrived at college with a lot of baggage—and not only the kind that can be carried in a suitcase. My mother had died just a couple of months before. And I hated my father—the town alcoholic—who had been abusive to my mother. But now I wanted to leave all that behind me. I wanted to make something of myself. I wanted to be happy and find meaning in life. I wanted the answers to three basic questions: *Who am I? Why am I here? Where am I going?* I had already given up on religion as holding any real answers to these kinds of questions, so I began to seek fulfillment in education. What a disappointment! I soon realized that the faculty members and my fellow students had just as many problems, frustrations, and unanswered questions as I had.

Around this time I became friends with a small group of Christians on campus. I admired them because they seemed to know where they were going in life, but I was openly skeptical about their faith. When they challenged me to examine the claims of Christ intellectually, I took them up on it. Determined to prove them wrong, I set out to make an intellectual joke of Christianity. But something happened that I didn't expect.

The more I researched, the more I became convinced that Christ had to be who He claimed to be. And that brought me to the inescapable realization that Jesus Christ loved me enough to die for me—sacrificing His life so I could have a relationship with God. The evidence helped me to see that Christianity was intellectually credible, but God's love made it relationally relevant to my life. So at the end of my second year of college, I surrendered my life to Jesus Christ.

Over the next eighteen months, my entire life was changed. God took my restlessness and gave me peace. He took away my desire to use people and gave me a desire to serve them instead. He helped me control my fiery temper—a problem I had struggled with for most of my life. But the most significant area of change in my life was the hatred and bitterness I felt toward my father. When I trusted Christ as Savior and Lord, the love of God inundated my life.

Five months after becoming a Christian, I found myself looking my dad right in the eye and saying, "Dad, I love you." Soon after, I had the privilege of leading my father to the Lord, something that I still consider one of the greatest joys of my life. Just fourteen months later, he died from complications of his alcoholism. But in that short time, more than a hundred people in the area around my hometown had committed their lives to Jesus Christ because of the change they saw in the town drunk, my dad.

The work God did in my life and the life of my father never ceases to fill my heart with wonder. People sometimes ask me if Christianity really works. I can say with confidence that it does, because Jesus Christ is in the business of changing lives. He certainly changed mine.

Now Josh is giving his life to confronting error and doubt with the transforming truth about Jesus and the Bible. You may have read his book, *Evidence That Demands a Verdict*. What is your verdict regarding the Bible and its message of hope in Christ?

"How long will you falter between two opinions? If the LORD is God, follow Him; but if Baal, follow him"
(1 Kings 18:21 NKJV).

36

SPIRITUAL VISION
James Merritt

Can a theater become a place of worship? Can a movie be a messenger of the gospel?

As a nine-year-old boy watching *King of Kings* in a movie theater, James Merritt "saw the light" that was to lead him to Christian maturity as a dynamic preacher, pastor of an evangelistic church, and leader of a great denomination. Now you can read in his own words the inspiring story of his initial life-changing experience and the incredible results.

I was saved as a nine-year old boy in, of all places, a movie theater! In August of 1962, I was watching the movie *King of Kings*. That movie depicted not only the life of Christ, but also His crucifixion. Sitting next to my mother in that darkened theater as I was witnessing Jesus being nailed to the cross, I asked myself in my heart, "Why are they doing that to Him? He never did anything wrong to anybody." The Lord (I now know) spoke to my heart and said, "*They* are not crucifying Him—you are." I responded in my heart, "Lord, I wasn't even there." The Lord spoke to my heart again and said, "Remember, He died for *your* sins."

Suddenly I saw the light. All that I had heard growing up in a Baptist church of how Jesus had died for me, and how He was raised from the dead, and how He came to save me made sense not only to my head but now to my heart. Sitting in that theater, in my heart I simply said a prayer like this: "Lord Jesus, I realize I am a sinner, and I'm lost, and I need to be saved, and I ask You to come into my heart and save me and forgive me of my sins." I turned to my mother and said, "Mother, I think I just got saved." My mom reacted with great shock and said, "We'll talk about it after we get home."

After we got home, my mother talked to me again, and just to make sure she prayed with me again to seal my relationship with Christ.

Quite frankly, when I asked Christ into my heart, I didn't hear angels sing. I didn't see bright lights. I didn't have goose bumps in the shape of doves running up and down my arm. In fact, I really did not *feel* anything. But I knew that the kid who walked out of that theater was not the same kid who walked in.

I will be forever grateful that the Lord Jesus loved me enough to come and die for me and called me unto Himself. I am grateful to God that He has given me this testimony, and I proclaim once again publicly and openly that Jesus Christ is my Lord.

In Their Own Words

The transforming power of trusting Christ as Savior came to James Merritt not as a dramatic spiritual explosion but as a deep, sincere relationship. He not only "saw the light," but he entered into a "know so" and "say so" relationship with the Son of God.

"For I determined not to know any thing among you, save Jesus Christ, and him crucified" (1 Cor. 2:2).

37

A SINNER WHO DIDN'T KNOW IT

R. Albert Mohler, Jr.

Sin is a condition of the heart. We don't become sinners by committing sins; we commit sin because, in our heart, we are sinners. God's Word tells us that, in His love for us, God sent His Son, Jesus, to die for our sin. He also sends the Holy Spirit to convince us that we are sinners in need of a Savior. Do you remember when God first convinced you that you were a sinner? Al Mohler, president of Southern Baptist Theological Seminary—one of the world's oldest, largest, and most respected seminaries—has vivid memories of the day he discovered he was a sinner.

Born into a Christian home, I never knew a time when I did not hear about Jesus. Godly Christian parents took me to every church event imaginable, and our church was such an important part of our family life that I could not conceive of life without it.

I was rocked in the nursery, listed on the Cradle Roll, scooted into Sunbeams, and lined up in the children's choir. Every Sunday I was taken to Sunday school, Training Union, and two worship services. On Wednesdays we ate dinner in the church social hall, went to prayer meeting, and then I joined other boys as Royal Ambassadors. Of course, none of this made me a Christian.

In fact, I was a sinner—lost and under the just condemnation of God for my sins. For several years I had no inkling that this was true. My parents talked about sin and sins, but I thought only of the latter. Beyond this I had observed my classmates sufficiently to judge myself fairly righteous. I had no idea I was lost.

Completing the fourth grade, I was informed that my home church would not be holding Vacation Bible School. Since I was almost certain that no summer could be authentic without VBS, my parents enrolled me in the Vacation Bible School organized by a small church not far from my school. It was not like my home church. Our church was large, had a cavernous sanctuary and a pipe organ, and called our pastor "Doctor," because he held the highest academic degree. The little neighborhood church, on the other hand, was a blue-collar congregation with particle board for walls, a small auditorium, an upright piano, and called its pastor "Brother."

Well, "Brother" pastor called all the children together on the last day of VBS for a final assembly. It was the first time he had talked to us himself. He delivered a stem-winder of an evangelistic message. I had never heard anything like it. He yelled and talked like a machine gun. He spoke of hell, sin, the devil, and just about everything else he could throw at us. I sat transfixed and afraid to breathe. For the first time I was forced to face the fact that I was—and am—a sinner. This meant not only that I had committed sins but that I was a sinner in grave peril. He told us that Jesus saves and that He would receive all who would come to him and believe. He warned that those who did not come to Jesus would be thrown into hell. He was quite specific about what hell was like. It was not a pretty picture. I felt like a spear had been thrust through my chest. I remember going home in a fog. I now know that was the convicting power of the Holy Spirit.

At home I found my mother and nervously tried to explain my predicament. My father, once home from work, joined the discussion. My parents talked me through the plan of salvation and then told me we would talk together with our pastor. Dr. T. Rupert Coleman sat in front of his giant desk in his formal office and explained the gospel to me in simple terms. He helped me to make my confession of Jesus Christ as Savior and Lord, and he explained that sinners find salvation through faith in Christ. He pointed me to the cross and explained that Jesus paid it all.

I was baptized the next Sunday night and left the next morning for Royal Ambassador camp. On the way I can remember thinking that the creaky church bus might wreck, but I would go to heaven. My theology was not very sophisticated, but I knew Jesus as my Savior.

I thank God for parents who taught me to love God. Thank God for that loud and faithful preacher who told me I was a sinner, and for that polished and educated pastor who sat down next to a trembling nine-year-old and carefully explained the gospel. God used both men to bring me to Christ. I am also thankful for that little church's determination to organize a Vacation Bible School. For at least one fourth-grader, it was nothing less than a road to Damascus, for there I met Jesus.

———

How did you respond when God revealed that you were a sinner in need of a Savior? Did you trust in Jesus, as Al Mohler did?

"To day if ye will hear his voice,
harden not your heart"
(Ps. 95:7–8).

38

YOUNG EARTH CREATIONIST

John Morris

After a youthful flight from God and godly parents, John Morris joined a tour to the Holy Land. Now you can read in his own words how Christ spoke to his rebellious heart as he stood at the very place where Jesus died for his sins. Faith in the risen Christ and the truth of the Bible has led him to challenge the secular skepticism of a materialistic culture.

God blessed me with a Christian home and godly parents who taught me the things of God from an early age. I was one of six children, so it was not often I was alone with my father. But one evening he arranged for all the others to be elsewhere in our small home. He reiterated the simple plan of salvation. As a child of six or so, I didn't understand all of Christian doctrine, but I did understand that I was a sinner and that Jesus Christ had died for my sins. I distinctly remember sitting in my father's lap as I asked God to forgive me of my sins and to make me His child. He responded with forgiveness and adoption into His family, and things have never been the same.

Unfortunately as a teenager and college student in the 1960s, I turned my back on Him. I never doubted the fact that I was His child, but I didn't want it. Graduating from college in Virginia, I took a job in Los Angeles to get as far away from godly influence as I possibly could. Thankfully God didn't abandon me, and He is alive and well in Southern California too. Through His prudence I met several people who were involved in the adventuresome search for Noah's ark. I was captivated and soon was included in the 1971 expedition.

In preparation for a vigorous climb, I quit doing a lot of things bachelors do. Meanwhile I felt it would be appropriate if I read the Bible. As the fog of sin lifted from my habits, the Bible began to make sense. It was even interesting! Unfortunately the expedition was cancelled, leaving me brokenhearted. On the rebound, I joined a tour of the Holy Land that included three days in Turkey at Mt. Ararat and the seven churches of Asia Minor. God was speaking to me, showing me just how accurate Scripture is, and that He wanted me to yield to His will.

We spent two weeks in Israel, visiting all the sites mentioned in Scripture. My resistance was breaking down. We ended up at Gordon's Calvary, a beautiful and serene possible site of the crucifixion. There's a bus station at its base, and the noise and fumes are distracting. But God helped me to shut it all out and focus on Him and the work of the cross.

It became so clear to me. Christ died! He died for me! His blood flowed down this hillside! Broken, I fell to my knees there at the foot of Calvary, and cried, "God, You have done it all. You've done it for me. Whatever I am, whatever I can be, I'm Yours. Take me and make me what You can. Use me in any way You choose. I'm Yours."

He graciously answered that prayer and has been so faithful. Following Him has truly been an adventure.

Back to Genesis expresses John Morris's challenge to any person who doubts the validity of the Bible. He challenges the doubter on the basis of sound scholarship to accept the fact that the Bible is truth.

"For Christ also suffered once for sins, the just for the unjust, that He might bring us to God, being put to death in the flesh but made alive by the Spirit" (1 Pet. 3:18 NKJV).

39

I HAD MISSED THE ESSENTIAL

Jim Murray

Jim Murray had joined the church, had learned to sing and pray, and had received recognition as a deacon. In short, he had done all the nonessentials but had missed the essential. Now you can read in his own words how he came to realize his need, how he humbly made his confession, how he entered into a living and real relationship with Jesus.

I was raised in a Christian home in Lansing, Michigan. At the age of thirteen, I went down and joined the church and got baptized. I have always been in church. The most comfortable place for me to be is in church. I began singing in a little local quartet called "The Melodaires" in Lansing. Upon graduating from high school, I moved to Detroit, Michigan, and began singing with a group called "The Orrell Quartet." It was during this time that I met Jake Hess, lead singer for "The Statesmen Quartet."

Jake said at some point that if he ever needed a tenor singer, he wanted to be able to call me. I was excited to think about traveling full-time with a group of such caliber as his new group, The Imperials.

Loretta and I got married in 1964 and moved out to Texas to begin our married life. After two years there, I got a call from Jake inviting me to come and sing tenor for The Imperials. We began by going to Del City, Oklahoma, to a Starlite Crusade sponsored by First Southern Baptist Church in Del City. Every summer we looked forward to coming to the Starlite Crusade and seeing all the good friends we had made over the years. In 1982, I was still singing with The Imperials, and First Southern asked me to come and close the last two nights of the giant crusade. Loretta and I went in a few nights early to spend time with our friends.

This particular night I wasn't singing but just sitting up in the bleachers. That night I heard a message that changed my life for eternity. Bailey Smith, pastor of First Southern at that time and preaching that night, delivered a message on Judas, which I thought was a strange subject for a message. He said something I had never thought of before. "Many of us are just like Judas. We kiss the Lord openly where everyone can see us, and yet down in the depths of our heart, we deny Him because He really isn't our Savior."

That was a new thought for me. Was it possible that I had been involved all of my life in the church and in singing gospel music, and still be lost? I knew how to pray a good-sounding prayer, and I could sing a good song for the Lord. In fact, I made my living singing gospel music. I had been ordained a deacon, taught Sunday school at one time, sung in the choir, and done all the things we all do when we are involved in a church.

But at that moment, I realized I had missed it totally! I'll never forget the choir as they sang, "The Savior is waiting to enter your heart." I swallowed my pride and walked down the stairs and out across the dusty track to the stage. Dr. LaFon came to me and asked me what we needed to pray about. I told him that I was a Judas. He looked at me with a strange face and said, "Well, if anyone knew the Lord, I thought you did."

I realized that I had never repented before the Lord and asked Him to forgive me for my sins and to cleanse me and give me strength to live for Him. That night I asked the Lord to save *me!* I'm so thankful that God is long-suffering and patient and gives us more opportunities than we deserve to come to know Him. The day of my salvation was July 7, 1982, at the Del City Starlite Crusade in the old football stadium. I can tell you " 'bout the time and I can take you to the place, where the Lord saved me by his wonderful grace! Praise His name!"

It is not easy to examine your real spiritual state on the basis of Bible standards. But the Bible says, "Examine yourself, whether you are in the faith." Are you ready to be completely honest with God?

> *"Except a man be born again, he cannot
> see the kingdom of God" (John 3:3).*

40

IN PRISON ... YET FREE

Manuel Noriega

Jesus said, "You shall know the truth and the truth shall make you free!" Later He said, "I am the truth!" Wherever men meet Jesus, they are set free . . . even in a prison cell. General Manuel Antonio Noriega was the powerful chief of Panama. Imagine the change in his life when suddenly he was arrested and imprisoned. But there in a prison cell he found true freedom through salvation in Christ. His testimony will remind you that *anyone* can be set free!

Before Christ came into my life, the realities of the materialistic world had the priority in my daily living. All of the past, together with illusions of grandeur, vainglory, and the priority of the "me world" over the "me spirit," with the heart hardened as those at Meribah (see Num. 20:1–13).

Before, Jesus to me was only an image of what was learned from traditions, a historic being who performed miracles. All was transformed when on Tuesday, January 16, 1990, Dr. Clift asked me in a telephone conversation—he in Texas and I in the preventive prison of the court—"Do you know that Jesus loves you?"

I received Jesus Christ as my Savior May 15, 1990, at 11:00 A.M. in a small room, like unto a cave, in the Metropolitan Correctional Center of Dade County, Florida, and under the inspiration and guidance of Dr. Clift Brannon and Rudy Hernandez in my condition as a prisoner.

Today this is what He means to me: He is the Son of God, who died on the cross for our sins, who arose from the grave, and is at the right hand of God the Father. Above all things, He is my Savior and has mercy on me, a sinner!

Many people feel imprisoned . . . limited by circumstances, events, past mistakes, and poor relationships. Wherever you are in life, even in circumstances like those of Manuel Noriega, Christ can set you free!

> *"Being then made free from sin, ye became the servants of righteousness" (Rom. 6:18).*

41

FINDING LIFE IN THE KILLING FIELDS

Sithon Nuon

It is difficult to imagine living in fear and starvation, wondering if you will live to see another day. In the midst of such circumstances, one man found life worth living when he found Christ as Savior. Read about the Buddhist who was born again.

I was born and raised in a Buddhist family in Cambodia. Under Communist regime (Khmer Rouge 1975–79), my parents and my brother were killed among those million people. One time near the end of 1975, I was taken to be killed too. Even though I was not a Christian, I prayed to God who could save my life. He saved my life indeed. Praise Him! In 1978, I was forced to marry a woman I had never seen before. In 1979, my wife was seven months pregnant. We escaped to the Thai border where later we got into a refugee camp.

In December of 1978, at work for the Lord who saved my life in 1975, He then saved my soul. Then I got involved in His work with the Southern Baptist missionaries (Rev. and Mrs. Dan Cobb). At the end of 1981, we were resettled in the Chicago area. There we attended and got involved in the Evangelical Christian Catholic Church affiliated with Moody Bible Institute.

In 1984, we moved to work in Chicago where we joined Uptown Baptist Church, Cambodian Mission, where I got trained under the leadership of Rev. Kevin Kane. In December 1988, the Lord called me to Jacksonville, Florida, to pastor the Cambodian Mission where I am now. The Lord is still using me to share His gospel with my people in Jacksonville, Florida, and also in my homeland (Cambodia).

In spite of the turmoil that may surround you, you can find peace when you come to know the Prince of Peace. Do you know Him?

"For the Son of man is come to
save that which was lost"
(Matt. 18:11).

42

BORN AGAIN ...
BEAT UP ... TO BECOME
A BLESSING

Stephen Olford

Saved as a teenager, Stephen Olford drifted into a life of carelessness and defeat. It took a severe injury from a motorcycle accident to bring him to the realization that God has incredible blessings in store for those who surrender to Him. A letter from his father triggered a fresh desire to yield completely to the Lord Jesus Christ. The result? A life that has touched millions.

I came to know Christ as my personal Savior as a boy of seven. It was a vivid and dramatic experience, so I have never had any occasion to doubt what happened on that memorable night. The circumstances stand out clearly in my mind. It was my birthday;

and as a special treat, mother had taken the family prayers. Reading from John 14, which speaks of the Savior's second coming, she closed our devotions by asking the question: "If Jesus were to come tonight, would you boys be ready?" I fought against such a thought as I went to bed, but the challenge persisted.

At midnight I could stand it no longer, so I called for my mother. Being in a deep sleep, she didn't answer me, and the horrifying thought struck me—Jesus had come, and I had been left behind! I called again, "Mother"... "Mother." And to my relief, she suddenly appeared. I shared my fears, and she led me simply and sweetly to a personal knowledge of Christ as the indwelling Lord and hope of glory.

At fourteen I was baptized, but it was not until the age of twenty-one that I came to realize the blessing of full salvation. I was saved all right but hopelessly defeated. I was saved but uselessly ineffective. I was saved but miserably unhappy. I was living a carnal, worldly life, and trying to convince my friends and myself that I was getting the best out of life. What was even more serious was that I was rebelling against God.

The Lord allowed me to undergo a serious accident that laid me on a deathbed. I was riding home from a motorcycle race meeting, having competed successfully. But in my bravado and unruliness, I skidded at high speed and was thrown to the road and lay there unconscious. When I was picked up after several hours, I was practically dead. The doctors gave me two weeks to live. During this period I fought with God and with myself. I refused to bend. I knew Jesus as Savior, but I refused to give Him sovereignty of my life as Lord. The battle was exhausting, and I was thinking day by day.

Then one unforgettable afternoon my mother brought in a letter from my father, who was still in central Africa. He had no idea of the life I was living or of my serious condition at that time, but, guided by the Holy Spirit, he wrote this message: "Stephen, my boy, this is most important, 'Only one life, 'twill soon be passed; only what is done for Jesus will last.'" Those words shattered me, and in a few minutes I was on my knees, imploring God for mercy and yielding my life to Christ as Lord and Master.

Instantly, a peace came into my soul, and I was given the sweet assurance of God's favor and blessing upon me. Not only did the Lord deliver me spiritually, but also He healed me physically, contrary to all medical expectation. I was wonderfully restored to full health and strength. In gratitude to my God, and in willingness to be used wholly and completely, I offered my life for the ministry, and a patient, loving Lord took me and has used me ever since.

There is a difference between knowing Jesus as Savior and Lord; it is the difference between life, and life more abundant. It is the difference between knowing peace *with* God and the peace *of* God which passeth all understanding. It is the difference between service that is a burden and service that is a blessing. Jesus must be Lord of all or not Lord at all. Is He Lord of your life?

In Their Own Words

Have you experienced abundant life in Christ? It comes only through yielding daily to His lordship.

"Why call ye me, Lord, Lord, and do not the things which I say?" (Luke 6:46).

43

WORLDS APART

Ron Owens
Patricia Owens

Known for their ministry in the United States and around the world, gifted vocalists and composers Ron and Patricia Owens came to know Christ on separate continents. God brought them together by first bringing them to Christ.

The crusade service arena in Schwennigen, Germany, had gone well. My father had preached, and I had, as I recall, sung a German translation of "I'd Rather Have Jesus." A number of people had responded to the invitation to repent of their sin and to receive Jesus Christ as their Savior.

When we returned to the Benzing house that night, however, as I climbed the steps to the little attic room above the clock factory where I slept, I was under deep conviction. Though I had grown up in a Christian home in eastern Canada and had heard the message of the gospel all my life (my father was a pioneer church planter/pastor), I had been living on my parents' faith. I was now sixteen; I knew the truth. But now, that night, it seemed as though I was hearing it for the first time. I knew I was lost.

During the hours of struggling and tears that followed, something interesting happened. I began thinking of my Grandfather Underhill who lived in Campbellton, New Brunswick, Canada.I remembered the times we had spent together playing. I remembered when he was working as head of the Campbellton street department how he would take me to work with him. I remembered how he loved me and talked to me about Jesus. I remembered how he seemed to love and care for the people who worked for him. I remembered how they seemed to really like him, andI remembered how proud I was to be his grandson.

I remembered him telling me one time how he wanted more than anything else to have Jesus be seen in him, and then I remembered how I suddenly wanted more than anything else to be like my grandfather. I remembered, and I knew what made him like he was. It was Jesus.

When I walked down those attic steps a few hours later, I was heading in a new direction. I had been going my way; I now was going God's way. I had turned around and had become what the Bible calls a new creation (2 Cor. 5:17). My grandfather was one, and I remembered. Years later I wrote a song about it.

I have been made a New Creation, with Christ I have
been crucified,

And what I was, I am no longer because I died when
Jesus died.

I have been made a New Creation, though I was part
of Adam's tree,

I now am grafted into Jesus, I am in Him and He's in
me.

I can't explain, it is a mystery, I don't know how it can
be true—

I just accept what He's accomplished; I'm born again,
all things are new.

Both Ron and Patricia benefited from a strong legacy of faith. Read
how Patricia's father was instrumental in her conversion.

The thing I first remember when I think about my coming to
know Jesus Christ as my Savior is the gift of faith that was present in
my home when I was a child—especially in the life of my dad. He
had a deep faith in the Lord, and I could tell that God was really
important to him. At home we always thanked God for our food and
sometimes at the breakfast table, Dad would read parts of the Bible
to us. Dad took the lead in seeing to it that our family was in church
every Sunday morning and evening, and my mother wanted this
also. As far back as I can remember, this was what we always did on
Sundays. I learned things about who God is at home and at church.

In Sunday school we were told about God's love in sending Jesus to save us from our sins. I learned that the reason there were times when I wanted to do things I knew were wrong was because my heart was sinful. I also learned that God hates sin because it separates people from Him. It was all these teachings from the Bible that God used in my life to make me uncomfortable about the wrong things in my heart and made me begin to long to have Him make things right inside.

I believed what the Bible said about Jesus being God's only begotten Son and that if I trusted Him He would give me everlasting life. Then one day I asked Jesus to forgive me and come into my heart and be my Savior. I was eight years old when I shared this with our pastor and church family.

There is a lot I can't remember about those moments, and I often have wished I could recall more about what was in my heart at that time—even that I could remember the exact day when I was "born of the Spirit." However, as a famous preacher, F. B. Meyer, has written, "We may remember the day and place of our new birth, or we may be as ignorant of them as of the circumstances of our natural birth. But what does it matter that a man cannot recall his birthday so long as he knows that he is alive?"

Thankfully, the one who brought about my new birth knows all the things I can't remember, and the Spirit of God makes me know that I am a child of God. How I praise Him! Knowing Jesus is the greatest treasure of my life. I find deep agreement with the hymn writer who expressed these thoughts:

And can it be that I should gain
An interest in the Savior's blood!
Died He for me, who caused his pain,
For me who Him to death pursued?
Amazing love! How can it be
That Thou, my God, should die for me?

Meeting Christ will put a new song in your heart. What song are you singing?

> *"I am crucified with Christ: nevertheless I live; yet not I, but Christ liveth in me: and the life which I now live in the flesh I live by the faith of the Son of God, who loved me, and gave himself for me"* (Gal. 2:20).

44

"KNOW SO" SALVATION
H. Franklin Paschall

Convicted, convinced, and converted at fourteen years of age, H. Franklin Paschall began his relationship with Christ. You can read in his own words how instruction and godly guidance matured his Christian life.

I was converted at age fourteen. Parental attention and instruction enabled me to avoid many pitfalls of youth. But I was a sinner and realized it.

Our family attended Oak Grove Baptist Church in Henry Country, Tennessee. The church was located in the northern part of the county near the Kentucky-Tennessee state line.

My Sunday school teacher was Mrs. Anis Orr, a saintly woman. All of the boys in the class were Christians except me. I did not want to make a false profession. My teacher would put her arm around me from time to time and say, "I am praying for you."

B. G. Arteburn was conducting revival services in the church. He was not a man of letters but one of the most effective evangelists I ever heard. During that revival I came under conviction and felt an urgent need to be right with God. It became crystal clear to me that Jesus was the perfect man and that God "hath made him to be sin for us, who knew no sin; that we might be made the righteousness of God in him" (2 Cor. 5:21). As the hymn says, "Jesus paid it all, / All to Him I owe; / Sin had left a crimson stain, / He washed it white as snow."

I trusted Him and Him alone to save me. A load was lifted, and the sky was studded with stars. It was a new beginning. I have a "know so" salvation. If one has salvation and doesn't know it, he can lose it and never miss it.

"Hallelujah! What a Savior."

———————

Franklin Paschall rejoices because Jesus cleansed the stains of sin and bestowed righteousness. Can you rejoice in a "know so" relationship with Christ?

"Jesus saith unto him, I am the way, the truth, and the life: no man cometh unto the Father, but by me" (John 14:6).

45

THREE QUESTIONS
Paige Patterson

In godly homes a child may become spiritually sensitive at an early age. You can read how three very crucial questions troubled Paige Patterson as a young boy. These questions were in regard to his personal salvation, his baptism, and his life's mission. In his own words, this Christian leader in theological education tells how he, though only a boy, found a satisfying answer that has enabled him to mature into an internationally recognized leader in ministry training.

Growing up in the godly home of a profoundly committed pastor resulted in early awareness of personal sinfulness and even a comprehension of what I needed to do in order to be saved. All of this I understood clearly by the age of six. People find it strange when I say, therefore, that the three most miserable and unhappy years of my life were between the ages of six, when I began to experience the convicting ministry of the Holy Spirit in my soul, and the age of nine, when I repented of my sin and looked to Jesus alone to save me.

During those three years I despised church. I was unalterably convinced that whoever wrote "Just As I Am" must have written at least forty-eight verses, and in public invitations the church was under some divine mandate to sing every verse. My mother made me sit by her during the time prior to my conversion, and she prayed for me with tears streaming down her cheeks in every invitation. I knew exactly what she was doing even though she never said.

The whole matter came to a head during a revival meeting at First Baptist Church of Beaumont, Texas, in April 1951. Fred Brown, well-known evangelist from Chattanooga, Tennessee, was preaching the revival. On Good Friday night, before Easter Sunday, I stood during the invitation with a death grip on the pew in front of me. I could not tell you what Evangelist Brown said, but I knew precisely that God was speaking to my heart. Somewhere in the process of the hymn being sung by the congregation, I remember it as though death would caress me and pull me to hell if I did not come to Christ instantly, and instantly I did exactly that.

I do not recall offering any kind of a specific prayer, and I am reasonably certain that I did not do so in any formal way, but as I took the first step out of the pew, my heart cried out to the living God. Before my foot reached the aisle, I knew beyond any shadow of a doubt that something so dramatic had happened in my heart that I would never forget it. Even today, nearly fifty years later, it is more vivid to me than anything that happened in the past week.

My father was the pastor of the church and was waiting at the front. I ran into his arms weeping so profusely that I could not speak. For what seemed like forever Dad simply held me as I wept from one eye tears of bitter repentance and from the other tears of gratification, relief, and release. Finally, Dad picked me up and carried me over and deposited me on the front pew. Looking into my eyes, knowing that I could not speak, he said, "Son, are you trusting Christ?" I nodded my head affirmatively. He continued, "Are you willing to follow Jesus in baptism?" Again, I nodded affirmatively. My dad knew there was no reason to spend time explaining this to me carefully at that moment since we had been over it so frequently before. He could tell by looking into my face what had happened.

But Dad did make one mistake. He failed to ask the third question. Following my baptism on Easter Sunday night, I again presented myself to the church on the following Wednesday night during prayer meeting. Dad was at first a bit confused and asked why I was returning during the invitation. I replied, "Because you did not ask the last question." "And what should the last question have been?" my dad asked. "You should have asked if I were committing my life to the ministry." My dad then asked the third question, and I responded that this was a part of my commitment at the time of my conversion. I knew then, as I know now, that I would have to spend my life telling everyone I could the story of what Christ had done in my life.

"When all else fails, read the instructions." Many people who struggle with crucial issues in life are overlooking the simple truths of God found in His Word. Have you turned to God's "instruction book"? Better yet, have you met the author?

"A wise son heareth his father's instruction"
(Prov. 13:1).

46

EVERYONE IN THE WORLD

Jerry Rankin

Here is the story of a boy blessed with godly parents and Christian influences. He experienced a new relationship with Christ that caused him to mature into an adult with a passion to evangelize lost people all over the world. Now you can read in his own words about the night God began in Jerry Rankin the life-changing experience that motivates his global mission.

I am grateful that God blessed me with godly parents who nurtured me in their Christian faith and centered our family life in church involvement that I might experience God's grace as a boy. When I was ten, several of my friends were "joining the church" and frequently asked when I was going to make a profession of faith and be baptized. I knew this was something

I needed to do and fully understood the importance of "being saved." After all, I had been in Sunday school all my life and won awards for Scripture memory! But something did not seem to be right, and the motivation for making a decision was lacking.

During that summer of 1952, a Billy Graham Crusade was held in Jackson, Mississippi, near where I lived, and our family attended faithfully. The message and appeal of Dr. Graham was so clear, and each night I would be filled with questions about what it meant. One night the message was on the consequence of sin. For the first time I understood with deep conviction that I was a sinner separated from God. I knew that Jesus had died on the cross to save sinners, but that night I felt that He died only for me. I prayed the sinner's prayer and then nudged my father and told him what I had done and asked if I could go forward in the invitation.

He took my hand and walked with me and my twin sister down those long stadium steps. When we reached the bottom and walked toward the counseling area, I was filled with a tremendous joy and sense of peace. I knew I had entered into a personal relationship with God that was secure for all eternity. In trying to identify a call of God that led me into missionary service, I find myself going all the way back to that salvation experience. Even now I recall thinking, *I wish everyone in the world could know Jesus,* as I came to know Him personally in that moment of trusting Him as my Savior and Lord.

An old hymn begins, "Rescue the perishing!" This becomes the life purpose of those who have themselves been rescued by Christ. Is this your song?

"And he said unto them, 'Go ye into all the world, and preach the gospel to every creature'" (Mark 16:15).

47

ADOPTED TWICE

Robert Reccord

The Bible says that believers are adopted into the family of God. In other words, God gave them the "once-over" and still loved and chose them in spite of their sin. Bob Reccord was adopted twice— first by an earthly family, then by the heavenly Father.

Life began very difficult. My natural mother died when I was six months old and left me and two older brothers with an alcoholic father. Things went from bad to worse until finally my brothers and I were split up, and I was adopted by a couple who could have no children. The young wife was a committed Christian, the husband a survivor from a tragic background himself who had been led to the Lord by his new, young wife.

Growing up in the home, I was taken to church every Sunday, went forward at age ten, became the president of my youth group, and was at the church every time the doors were open (largely due to the continuing prodding of my adoptive mother). While I knew all the facts, there was one key thing I did not know—Christ, personally.

Going away to Indiana University, I charted a course of rebellion, getting involved in activities and attitudes that I knew would break my parents' hearts. Despite having been on a scholarship to study for medical school, it did not take me long to lose the scholarship and my "graduation with honors" status from high school.

In the midst of my wrong activities and attitudes, a Campus Crusade for Christ staff member continually tried to share Christ with me. I did everything in the world to avoid him. But every time he saw me, he left me with the sobering thought, "Bob, God loves you where you are, but he loves you too much to let you stay there."

One night after a campus party that had gone bad, I found myself very sick. I realized I wasn't having nearly the fun that everybody told me I was having. At that moment the phrase about God's love came crashing into my thought processes. So it was at 2:00 in the morning on May 8, 1970, that I entered into a personal relationship with Jesus Christ . . . and life has never been the same since! It was a decision that would lead to the one who would become my wife, a new direction for my life, and a deep gratitude that God, indeed, loved me where I was, *but too much to let me stay there!*

We all need to be adopted at least once. Have you experienced the grace of God and been adopted into His glory?

"For ye have not received the spirit of bondage again to fear; but ye have received the Spirit of adoption, whereby we cry, Abba, Father" (Rom. 8:15).

48

A GAMBLER'S BEST DEAL

Chip Reynolds

Pool was his sport; beer was his drink; chance was his master; lust was his business; money was his goal; Miss Go-Go was his girl-friend. How could such a mature addict to sin find the good life? Let Chip tell his secret.

I was a nightclub owner and living with a go-go dancer, gambling on everything, and living the "if it feels good do it" so-called dream life. My life was filled with immorality, greed, and an "I don't care" attitude. I had all the world's toys, but none had any lasting satisfaction.

My mother had multiple marriages, so I had no father to look up to. The YMCA became a father figure for me. They were men who cared about my life and taught me all about sports. One I became fairly good at was pool. I won the annual pool tournament at the age of twelve. I started gambling in poolrooms, which led to nightclubs. At the age of twenty, I went into partnership, in a nightclub with beer and go-go girls.

I was making a lot of easy money from the club and gambling. I was in that business for six years and owned five different nightclubs. I met my future wife in the clubs when she came to work for me as a go-go dancer. She was Miss Go-Go of Tulsa in 1975.

We got tired of all the late-night lifestyle, so I sold my clubs and got a real-estate license to make a living. Through my real-estate dealings we were invited to Eastwood Baptist Church in Tulsa, Oklahoma. We came to meet new people, but God had other plans. The Bible became alive for me. Jane and I, who were not married but living together at the time, went to church every time the door was open. After a couple of weeks, we made an appointment with Pastor Tom Elliff to find out how to join the church. He shared with me the simple gospel message of Jesus' love for me and how I could become a Christian. Still having a gambling frame of mind, I said this was the greatest deal in the world.

I opened my heart that day in 1977 and received Jesus as my Savior. The huge flood of sin in my life was gone. I felt clean and forgiven. Jane, being an atheist at the time, didn't accept Jesus, but in about three weeks she also received Jesus as her Savior. By the way, we were married three days after I got saved. God saved Jane's mom, my mom, some friends, and eventually all seven of our children. I am now in full-time Christian ministry as an associate pastor at the church I was saved in. Instead of pouring beer at a bar,

I am sharing Jesus with people, the one who can really help their lives.

Chip proves that God will do the impossible if a person will only trust Him. There are no sins so big that God cannot save you. Neither are there any sins so small that it does not take faith in Christ to experience forgiveness.

"Sirs, what must I do to be saved? And they said, Believe on the Lord Jesus Christ, and thou shalt be saved, and thy house" (Acts 16:30–31).

49

CONVICTED AS A CHILD

R. Philip Roberts

Phil Roberts had the normal curiosities and interests of any young child. But one day there developed in him a growing conviction that he needed to be saved. Now you can read of his life-changing experience with Christ.

It was my joy and privilege to have been raised in a Baptist preacher's home. From the beginning I was nurtured in the things of God. Attending Sunday school and church were a regular part of my life. Beginning at age five or six, I distinctly remember being convicted of my need for Jesus Christ. In fact, many times at church while hearing the gospel preached, I sensed that I needed the forgiveness of God and a personal relationship with Jesus Christ! It was clear to me that I was a sinner, even if not a very experienced one, and that God loved me so much that Jesus Christ died for my sins.

One Sunday evening as my father was preaching a revival meeting at our small pioneer church in Columbus, Ohio, God clearly touched my heart and life. He showed me that if I were to die I would be responsible for having consciously rejected the gospel. At that point my heart was broken. I broke out in tears and with the encouragement of my mother went forward to make my faith in Jesus Christ known publicly.

Looking back on all the events, I can honestly say that giving my life to Christ was the greatest and most important decision of my life. Nothing has impacted me, nor ever will, like surrendering my all to Jesus. He has assured me of a home in heaven and has been the guiding light in all my decisions. I have the daily fellowship and relationship with Jesus that surpasses all of life's other wonderful blessings. If all of life's pleasures were taken from me, knowing Jesus would still fill me with joy.

Many mature adults will point to their early decision for Christ as being the most important and formative decision in their lives. Isn't it time you made that decision?

"But the LORD said unto me, Say not, I am a child: for thou shalt go to all that I shall send thee, and whatsoever I command thee thou shalt speak" (Jer. 1:7).

50

MY DADDY PRAYED WITH ME

Darrell Robinson

Now you can read about a boy who loved livestock and was not a talker. Yet he grew into a man who loves God. Now he won't stop talking. Read about this truly life-changing experience.

The least likely thing that I can imagine is that Darrell Robinson is a preacher. I never intended to be a preacher or pastor. The height of my ambition was to be a veterinarian and a cattle rancher. I planned to go to Texas A&M and get a degree in veterinary medicine and make enough money to buy a ranch. I loved livestock. I did not have to talk to them, and I was not a talker. My wife asks, "What happened to you? Now all you do is talk."

God knew me better than I knew myself! He called me to preach and surfaced the gifts in my life to obey and be used by

Him. I would still enjoy ranch life, but I am glad I yielded to God and did what He said. If I had not, I would have missed out on the greatest adventure my life could have known—that of placing my hand in the hand of the Lord and walking with Him.

During my early life our family did not go to church much. My dad worked hard and often seven days a week to make a living. My parents were Christians, but I did not know it. They had been saved during their youth. When they married and I came along, they got out of church. They simply assumed that I knew what they knew about spiritual things without ever having been taught. Many parents make that mistake.

But we did go to church during summer revivals. I would sit as far back as I could get and listen to as little as I could, because the whole thing bothered me. I knew I needed Jesus. I was lost and was on my way to hell. Many nights before I went to sleep I would pray silently and ask God to forgive me and save me, but I never had assurance that He did.

One night when I was thirteen years old, God dealt strongly with me at one of those revivals. On the way home my mother said, "Darrell, didn't you want to be saved tonight?"

I wondered, *What does she know about that?* But I answered, "Yes, I did!"

She responded, "You think about it tonight, and in the morning your dad will talk to you about it." I was terrified. I had no idea Daddy was a Christian. I was afraid to pray, to walk an aisle in that big church with at least forty to fifty people. I was afraid of baptism. The preacher might drown me!

The next morning my dad took me in the bedroom. We got on our knees! He was as afraid as I was. His voice trembled when he spoke. He told me that Christ died on the cross for me and rose again. He said that Jesus would come into my heart and save me if I could repent of my sins and ask Him to forgive me and come into my life. He asked me to pray!

I was too scared. I could not open my mouth! Then I heard my dad begin to pray for me, and I opened my heart and received Jesus, praying silently. That was the first time I had ever heard my daddy pray. Spiritual things were foreign to us. He is in heaven now. When he died, he left me a lot of things—land, money, and other things. But the best thing he left me was the memory of a dad who prayed for me and showed me how to receive Christ and be saved.

That night I confessed Christ, and on Sunday night I was baptized. I was afraid of water, but I would have done it if the preacher had drowned me. That is what Jesus said do, and I knew I must obey Him. I had received Him! He is my Lord! He has never let me down. He impressed on my heart that I must "live as a dying man" (Gal. 2:20). I am more than a conqueror through Him who loved me (Rom. 8:37).

What if every dad were to decide to pray with his children? Have your children enjoyed this privilege with their dad and mom?

"The righteous man walks in his integrity; his children are blessed after him" (Prov. 20:7 NKJV).

51

ONE LOVE WORTH FINDING

Adrian Rogers

The pastor of a megachurch, a national voice for religion, a radio personality who tells millions of listeners about the "one love worth finding" now shares in his own words the beginning of his relationship with the love of Christ.

I was reared in a nonchurchgoing home. My parents were decent, hardworking people, but church was not a part of our lives. Someone invited my father to a revival crusade when I was a teenager. We attended as a family. I was sitting next to my father when he stepped out to give his heart to Christ. I knew that I needed the Lord and stepped out with him. Before that time I had a great disquiet in my heart. I had been guilty of schoolyard fights, bad language, truancy, and cheating in school. I knew that my life was not right with God, but I did not know how to be saved.

In that revival crusade the people had me fill out a card which said basically that I was coming to profess my faith in Christ and to be baptized. That was true, but I was not instructed in how to have assurance of salvation.

For about a year and a half I was on a spiritual roller coaster. I was not living in victory. Sometimes I would think that I was lost, and the Holy Spirit had me under conviction. At other times I would think that I was saved, and the devil was trying to make me doubt it.

Finally, one day after I had walked my girlfriend home, I stopped about one block from her house and looked up into the sky and prayed a prayer something like this: "God, I need You. I don't have peace in my heart. I don't know whether I am saved and filled with doubt or that I have never been saved, but I want to settle it right now. I now understand that salvation is totally by grace. Therefore, once and for all, now and forever I ask You to save me. I receive You into my heart as my Lord and my Savior. I give all there is of me to You. I don't ask You for a sign, and I don't look for a feeling. I stand on Your Word. You cannot lie. You are now my Lord, my Savior, my God, and my friend. Thank You for doing it."

When I prayed that prayer, all of the doubts left, and they have been banished from that time on. From that moment until now, I have had a desire to share Jesus with other people.

Jesus Christ is real to me. He is not someone whom I know

about but someone whom I know and love with all of my heart. Praise Him forevermore.

―――――――――――

The essence of faith is taking God at His word. Have you done that?

"Hereby know we that we dwell in him, and he in us, because he hath given us of his Spirit" (1 John 4:13).

52

PREACHER DAD/ PREACHER SON

Bailey Smith

Two ministers were speaking of their church service on the previous Sunday. "Two and a half people came to know Christ," said one. "Oh," said his friend, "I suppose you mean two adults and one child?" "No," his friend responded, "I mean two children with their whole life ahead of them and one adult with less than half a life to live." Here is the testimony of one who was saved at an early age. What began as a childhood conviction at five climaxed as a firm decision at ten. Now Bailey Smith, famous evangelist, records the story of his initial experience with Jesus Christ as Savior and Lord. In his own words you can read the influences that led Bailey Smith to his firm faith in the gospel messages he has preached to multitudes.

At five years of age, I went forward at my grandfather's church to get saved. I was later baptized. However, five years later in a revival meeting preached by Roy Kemp, an independent Baptist evangelist, I truly was born again and followed this true decision with a true baptism.

The revival was in 1949, at the Elam Baptist Church in East Dallas, Texas, where my dad, B. E. Smith was pastor. Eight years later, I walked the aisle to tell my dad I was "called to preach."

───────────

Bailey Smith's experience shows the difference between "going forward" and the reality of being "born again." Have you experienced this new birth by the power of the Holy Spirit?

"These things have I written unto you that believe on the name of the Son of God; that ye may know that ye have eternal life" (1 John 5:13).

53

A VOICE IS STILLED

J. Harold Smith

J. Harold Smith deserves recognition as one of the leading evangelists of this generation. Like David, he won "tens of thousands." And God gave him a long life of more than ninety years. When requested, he sent his brief testimony of his salvation when he was a young man. This record is a vital page in the irreplaceable story of his life. This brief account is a record of the most important experience God ever gave. Notice how he shares the circumstances, the influences, the personal faith, and the God-given results of his salvation. He goes beyond the fact of his salvation and helps all who read to see the path he walked to receive the Savior. Now read his last testimony. J. Harold Smith went to be with his Lord shortly after writing this account.

Sunday, September 4, 1932, was a beautiful day I will never forget. My oldest sister, Mildred, lived just back of my mother and dad on Owens Street in Greenville, South Carolina. I had gone down the little path that led from my mother's back door to Mildred's back door to visit her husband and her for a few minutes.

I was sitting on her front porch with my feet propped up on the banister that bordered her porch. She and her husband were sitting in the porch swing, when right out of the blue she said, "Harold, you have tried everything the devil has to offer. Why don't you give Jesus Christ a chance in your heart?" I really snapped to attention when she said that, and anger filled my heart. I turned to look at her, and when I did, I saw the tears streaming from her eyes. I knew if anyone in all the world loved me, it was my oldest sister.

I did not know there was such a person as the blessed Holy Spirit, but He took those tears and broke my heart. I did not know a verse of Scripture. I had never prayed a prayer in all my life. The Holy Spirit led me to say, "Lord Jesus, have mercy on me, and forgive me of all my sins." Jesus came to where I was and entered into my heart, and I knew in a moment that every sin I had ever committed was under His precious blood. I was born into the kingdom of God. Before I stood up, while still on my knees, the Holy Spirit said, "Will you now surrender to preach the gospel of Christ?"

I came up off my knees, a child of the king and a preacher of the gospel of Christ. On June 14, 2001, I will celebrate my ninety-first birthday, and I have preached more than sixty-eight thousand times. God has been so good to me these sixty-eight years of my ministry! That was my greatest hour.

Suppose today were to be your last. Do you have the confidence like J. Harold Smith that you would spend your forever in heaven with God?

"No man can come to me, except the Father which hath sent me draw him" (John 6:44).

54

DAD'S MIRACLE

Ruffin Snow

This is the story of what a miracle for Dad did for his son. Mother had taken the son to church and Sunday school, but the miracle that God worked in Dad's life brought conviction. Now you can read in his own words how Ruffin Snow in his boyhood so witnessed how the saving power of Jesus did the impossible in his father's life that he was convicted of his own spiritual need and came to his own life-changing experience.

Our Lord is so gracious. When I was a child in the late 1940s, church attendance was not a part of our family's life. My mother would take me to church occasionally, but my dad would never go. Mom was a Christian, and Dad was a lost alcoholic. My earliest vivid memory is of going with Mom to pick Dad up at a beer joint when some other men got into a fight in the parking lot. All the yelling and blood and broken beer bottles used as weapons left an indelible impression on my mind.

We lived for a while in what I later realized was a very poor section of Bartlesville, Oklahoma. A sweet lady in a big station wagon would come through our neighborhood picking up children like me and taking them to Vacation Bible School at the First Baptist Church. My mother joined that church, and she and I and my new baby brother attended there for a time. I remember the Sunday school teacher suggesting that I get Dad to come with us to church. "Oh, he couldn't do that," I sincerely replied. "He's always sick on Sunday morning." It seemed totally logical to me.

By God's grace, we moved to Wichita, Kansas, in 1952, where some hardy believers were starting the Sharon Baptist Church in the apartment of a fireman, Mr. Nichols, and his wife Velma. Mr. Nichols and some other men camped on our doorstep until they succeeded in getting my dad to come to church. There he became convicted and received Christ as Savior and Lord. He was a man who woke up each morning thinking about alcohol, and yet he stopped drinking immediately, never to take it up again. Our family was totally changed, and my mother and I were so happy.

Although it was visibly awkward to him at first, Dad began reading the Bible to us and praying each evening. The pastor had said that men ought to do this, so he did it. During one of these family devotions, I asked my parents how I could be saved. Little wonder that I would ask, since there had been such obvious changes in our family. It embarrasses my folks now, but their immediate response was, "Oh, Ruffin, you probably don't need to be saved."

But I knew very well that I did need it, and I continued to nag about the subject. Finally they asked the pastor, Rang Morgan, to come to our house and share the gospel with me. I didn't receive Christ at that time, but a week or so later on a Sunday afternoon, sitting in Dad's pickup at a job site, I made my decision. That night at church I could barely wait for the invitation. When it finally began, I marched down the aisle and there invited Christ into my heart. When Brother Rang asked me what I had done, I said, "I gave my heart to Jesus." It was a week before my seventh birthday. I was baptized two weeks later in a borrowed baptistry. Not all seven-year-olds are ready for conversion, but I know I was. "Salvation is of the Lord."

What a challenge to fathers to lead their children to know Jesus because of the example in their own lives. What are you doing for your own children?

"The just man walketh in his integrity: his children are blessed after him" (Prov. 20:7).

55

RENEW YOUR MIND

R. C. Sproul

R. C. Sproul is a scholar who loves to help people understand the significance of their beliefs. He calls it "renewing your mind." While he does not force his beliefs on others, he is persuasive and convincing. Now you can read in his own words about his personal relationship with Christ and his faith in his Lord.

Growing up, sports were my life. In high school, at the age of sixteen, I learned that my father had an incurable disease, and I was enraged. This was the first time I had faced an unsolvable problem. When we buried my dad, my soul went under with him. The next year was a year of unrestrained degeneracy. I became the paradigm of the angry young man.

The following year I attended college. One week on campus and my life was turned upside down again. The star of the football team called me aside and told me about Jesus. I couldn't believe this guy. In my eyes ministers were "pansies," and *Christian* was a synonym for *sissy*. I don't remember exactly what he said to me, but it drove me to the New Testament. Truth breathed from every page. It was my virgin experience with the Bible. It was a spiritual experience of revolution. I always knew there was a God, but I hated Him. In this week my anger and bitterness dissolved into repentance. The result was forgiveness and life.

The more I study and the more I teach and engage in dialogue with unbelievers and critics, the more confident I have become in the rock-solid intellectual integrity and truth of Christianity. In fact, I am overwhelmed by the profundity, coherency, and intricate internal consistency of Christianity. I am awed by the majesty and brilliance, as well as the power, of the Scriptures. Take away the Scriptures and you take away Christ. Take away Christ and you take away life. My conviction is one with that of Luther: *Spiritus Sanctus non est scepticus:* "The Holy Spirit is not a skeptic, and the assertions He has given us are surer and more certain than sense and life itself."

The Christian faith and its textbook, the Bible, can withstand the assaults of any criticism. In an era of uncertainty, isn't it encouraging to know that God is a God of absolute truth?

"And be not conformed to this world: but be ye transformed by the renewing of your mind, that ye may prove what is that good, and acceptable, and perfect, will of God" (Rom. 12:2).

56

FIRST TIME WAS ENOUGH

John Sullivan

From a West Virginia coal mine to FBI headquarters seems an impossible leap. What happened next is even more incredible. Newly married to Nancy, he agreed to go to church with her the next Sunday. Then it really began! Read in John Sullivan's own words how he responded to the gospel call on his first visit to church and his first hearing of salvation in Christ. As you read, you will learn the initial experience that has led to his present aggressive ministry of leadership in the work of the Lord Jesus.

Growing up in the coal camps of West Virginia was often more conducive to survival than salvation. My parents were good, moral, and industrious but not church-minded. My father taught me how to work, and my mother taught me how to think. Neither survived long enough to see grandchildren. Mother died at thirty-six years of age, Dad at forty-seven.

Seventeen is young to leave a small coal-mining town and move to "the far country." A high school principal believed in me and recommended me for an intern position with the FBI in Washington, D.C. To say I was elated to receive a letter from J. Edgar Hoover offering me the position would be a major understatement. It was the opportunity of a lifetime for me. This decision would prove the most critical of my life.

When my father left me at a boardinghouse in D.C., I had my letter from Mr. Hoover, enough money for a month's room and board, and an empty feeling about the unknown qualities of the big city.

Not long after moving to D.C., I met Nancy, a deacon's daughter from Arkansas. We started dating—nothing serious at first. She was different from others I had dated. She was the first person to witness to me about Jesus. At least I don't remember anyone else witnessing to me. If they had, it had not helped! There was no pretense on my part about being religious. I was lost and lived like it.

Soon I realized my love for Nancy had grown to the extent that I wanted her to be my wife. So at eighteen on June 24, 1955, we married. We both continued our employment with the FBI.

One Monday in August 1955, Nancy invited me to church the next Sunday. It was good timing and I agreed. By Wednesday, I wondered why. By Friday I was angry. However, my anger was no match for her sweet, persistent "you promised." A foreign missionary, whose name I do not know, preached a sermon that I cannot recall, from a Bible passage that seemed unimportant. But then they sang, "Have Thine Own Way," which I do remember!

It was awkward explaining to the pastor that Sunday morning what was happening. Nothing like this was in my experience. Pastor Al Smith helped me to understand what Nancy had been telling me. On the spot I invited Jesus into my life. And He came! It was nothing I did. It was nothing I had joined! It was not my knowledge of Scripture. Before my conversion the Bible was not a part of my reading program. I did not even own one. It was His love.

What a wonderful day it was. First time in my adult life to be in church. First time anyone had told me what to do. First time ever to "go forward." My life has never been the same! Jesus saved me!

————————

Though John Sullivan had the insight to respond to his first hearing of the gospel, some who read his wonderful account will have heard many times and never responded. What is your response?

"Now when they heard this, they were pricked in their heart, and said . . . what shall we do?" (Acts 2:37).

57

HAPPY DAY
Jack Taylor

Millions search and strive and work and spend in a vain effort to find happiness. Failure is assured because they seek happiness in the wrong places and by the wrong methods. In his own words, Jack Taylor tells how as a boy he yielded to the conviction of the Holy Spirit, received Jesus as his Savior, and began a new life in Christ that has borne happiness through every era of his life.

I grew up in a rural area of the Texas Panhandle. The major spiritual influences in my life were my mother, faithful to take her children to church, the church to which she would take us, and a praying aunt who lived a few hundred yards from our little farm home.

When I was ten years old, the culturally appointed age for children in our community to "join the church," the annual revival meeting came about. During the days of that meeting, two of my friends and I were discussing what we needed to do and, after the discussion, simply resolved to do it. I remember no conviction of sin or emotion during the discussion. However, between the discussion and actual public decision there was some serious awareness of sin on my part and a heavy sense of seriousness about what we were going to do. We had chosen a morning service of the revival meeting (a time when fewer folks would be in attendance) to make our professions of faith.

When the invitation was given after the message, the other two boys resolutely marched forward, but I lingered behind a few minutes. Somehow I knew that if this decision did not go past my mind and into my heart, it would be without meaning. Finally, as conviction mounted, I walked forward, declaring that I was accepting Jesus as my personal Savior.

My memories have faded across the years about folks present and feelings I had, but one thing remains as clear as if it had taken place this morning. That was the chorus of the song they sang as people came by to congratulate us on our decisions:

The song is "O Happy Day." The chorus I well remember says:

> O happy day, happy day,
> When Jesus washed my sins away.
> He taught me how to watch and pray
> And live rejoicing every day.
> Oh happy day, happy day,
> When Jesus washed my sins away.

After all these years the words of the song ring true in every era of life. It was indeed a "happy day."

No person who has surrendered to Jesus has ever failed to find life—and that more abundantly—because this is what Jesus alone is able to give. Have you trusted Jesus as your Savior and Lord?

"I am come that they might have life, and that they might have it more abundantly" (John 10:10b).

58

CLEAN!
Mark Trammell

As a nationally known Christian vocalist, Mark Trammell was constantly exposed to gospel music and preaching. But you don't become clean by standing next to a tub of water. Read Mark's testimony of what it took for him to become really clean.

Four and a half months after hearing Dr. Bailey Smith's sermon on "Wheat and Tares" at a Starlite Crusade in Spartanburg, South Carolina, God sat me down in the First Southern Baptist Church in Del City, Oklahoma, to hear Dr. Tom Elliff give the first point to a sermon titled "Build an Ark and Save Your Home." Being the youngest of four Baptist preacher's kids, I found myself realizing that religion had burned out and Jesus was just in my head and not living in my heart.

So on July 13, 1988, at the third tee box of the Willow Creek golf course, I asked Dr. Elliff to place his hand on my chest. My heart was about to explode. I told him that I knew God was telling me that I was lost. Dr. Elliff's first sermon point had been, "Settle the question of your salvation." I couldn't get past that. From the moment I heard him make that point to the moment we got on our knees at that tee box seemed like an eternity, yet it was only two days. Dr. Elliff and I knelt at a bench there, and he led me through the sinner's prayer, and Jesus gloriously saved me that day. I was dirty on the outside from kneeling on an area where the golf course had been watered earlier that day. But for the first time in my life, I was *clean* on the inside! Praise God.

A great gospel songwriter wrote a song that fits me perfectly. The chorus says, "Saved like a drowning man, / pulled from the sea. / Saved like a prisoner from captivity. / Saved like an outcast with a new family, / I'm saved by the blood of the lamb. / I am saved by the blood of the lamb."

Many people come regularly to the edge of the gospel rim without crossing over through repentance and faith. On which side of that river do you stand?

"Examine yourselves, whether ye be in the faith;
prove your own selves" (2 Cor. 13:5a).

59

THE MINISTRY OF TEARS

Jerry Vines

A few simple experiences were used by God to bring Jerry Vines to Christ:

- A friend invited
- A Christian explained
- A man of God preached
- A sinner responded

Now you can read in his own words of the sequence that led Jerry Vines to Jesus.

I came to know Jesus as my personal Lord and Savior at the age of nine. On a Sunday afternoon a friend of mine told me he was going to church that night and was going to join the church.

He wanted to know if I wanted to go with him. I agreed to go, not knowing what to expect. I recall going to the pastor's office before the service. There he told me the story of Jesus.

I went into the Sunday evening service and sat on the second row down front. As God's man faithfully preached the Word, I saw tears rolling down his cheeks. The Holy Spirit used his compassion to touch my heart, convict me of my sin, and show me my need of Christ. When the invitation was given, I went forward, giving my hand to the preacher and my heart to Jesus. Although I didn't know a great deal of what was involved at the time, I did know I was a new boy. Old things had passed away; I was now a new person in Christ!

———————————

This dedicated pastor and his great church continue to use these simple methods to lead the lost to the Savior. Are you using the simple gospel message to win the lost?

"He that goeth forth and weepeth, bearing precious seed, shall doubtless come again with rejoicing, bringing his sheaves with him" (Ps. 126:6).

60

THE DEAF "HEAR"

Larry White

As the deaf pastor of a deaf congregation, Larry White speaks to his people with expressive face and nimble hands by the "signs" that communicate the glorious gospel of Jesus Christ. His people "hear" by seeing. Their fellowship glows with silent praise and radiant communion. Their joy shines on their faces. Now you can read the wonderful story of the life-changing experience that led Larry to this rewarding field of service.

I remember as a young boy attending church, I would watch people going to the pastor during the invitation. I always wondered what they were talking about. Most of my family and relatives who are deaf and Christian attend deaf church regularly. Assuming that I was a Christian, because of my mother, aunt, uncle, and cousins being Christians and members of the deaf church, I thought I would become a member too. I went to the pastor and asked if I could join the church. I was twelve years old when I was baptized.

I still attended church regularly with all of my family and relatives. But when I started college, I began to examine my life's faith seriously. I looked back to my childhood experience with God, trying to remember my salvation experience. I had been in a church for a long time and had always been labeled as a "good boy." I finally confessed and prayed to receive Jesus in my heart one Wednesday after the chapel service at college. At that time I really experienced totally life-changing salvation.

Jesus Christ now lives in my heart forever. I am saved through Jesus, not by baptism or by my family being Christian or by faithful church attendance. I claim Ephesians 3:8–9 as a testimony promise from God's Word along with my salvation experience.

———————

The crucial moment arrived when Larry saw the reality of life that comes by faith in Jesus Christ. He heard by seeing; have you seen by hearing?

> *"So then faith cometh by hearing, and hearing by the word of God" (Rom. 10:17).*

61

TESTIMONIES OF THEIR OWN

Robert Gee Witty
Tom Elliff

Your testimony is just that; it is your testimony. There is none other in the world exactly like yours. Once two noted athletes were asked to share their testimonies at a banquet. One of the men shared a simple and moving testimony of his encounter with Christ. When the other was called upon to speak, he stood and said, "Mine is just like his!"

Well, no testimony is exactly like another. In fact, the second man later spent time in prison where he was introduced to Christ. Now he has his own personal testimony.

In this chapter the authors of this book would like to share with you their testimonies, in their own words. First, read the testimony of Robert Gee Witty.

I was born and raised in Glasgow, Kentucky. My home was strongly Christian: a godly mother, two godly grandmothers, and a godly grandfather. Our church was an old-fashioned Southern Methodist in which I heard both the gospel preached and testimonies of salvation.

When I was about seven, I began to feel conviction of sin. The evangelistic preaching, the prayers of my mother, and the warmhearted testimonies increased the spiritual concern. I still remember how the testimonies of Mr. Hill and Mr. Minick were given to the Sunday school with tears of joy coursing down their faces. I began to fear that I would go to hell. This grew until I was eight. I was in the service with my grandfather, and the Lord definitely constrained me to respond.

Leaving my seat, I went forward and asked the preacher, "What must I do to be saved?"

"Kneel here at the altar, ask God to forgive you, and ask Jesus to come into your heart."

I knelt weeping and prayed for salvation. I don't remember what I said, but I do remember that peace came to me. I remember that the sun shone through the picture of Jesus in the window more beautifully than I had ever seen it. Fear left me, and peace came to me.

Shortly after that we had a revival, and though I knew nothing about soul-winning, I persuaded my friend, Porter Dilley, to go up and give his heart to Jesus. Though I had no contact with Porter since childhood, I recently received an E-mail from his grandson wanting to know about his deceased grandfather and his salvation.

Through the years God has been faithful even though I do not deserve His mercy. I rejoice and thank God for my salvation.

———————————

Robert Witty was blessed by being reared in a home where Christ was loved and respected. Such was the case with the second author, Tom Elliff. Read about the impact of both a godly heritage and the work of the Holy Spirit in an outdoor revival.

———————————

My testimony is positive proof that going to church will not guarantee you a place in heaven. I was raised in a solidly Christian home, both the son and the grandson of Baptist preachers. In fact, from my grandfather forward there are seventeen preachers in our family. My mother also came from a God-fearing home. She was the youngest of eleven, all of whom served the Lord, passing on their faith to subsequent generations.

I never remember a time when I was not in church. Nor do I ever remember a time when I rebelled against the practice of attending church. As one man said, "It just came naturally in our family." In the summer of 1951, as a seven-year-old boy, I met Christ during a summer outdoor crusade in Fordyce, Arkansas.

Excitement was in the air as we anticipated the arrival of the evangelist for our summer crusade. This would be an outdoor crusade with a genuine sawdust trail . . . the first such meeting my preacher father had scheduled at the First Baptist Church. I can still remember how enthusiastic I was about spreading the word. A great banner was swung across the street by the church. My friends and I rode our bicycles around town, passing out flyers, and nailing small posters to trees and fence posts. When our supply ran out, I remember taking small scraps of paper and writing "Revival!" then nailing them to the trees. Little did I realize the truth of the statement that "we receive out of something in direct proportion to what we put into it." I was about to receive the greatest gift of eternity.

Each night I sat transfixed as the evangelist fervently preached the gospel from a wood platform over which yellow lights had been strung. At invitation time I would start down the sawdust trail, but fear would always overtake me. Instead, I would slide into the nearest bench. Finally after arriving home on Thursday night, I told my mother I just couldn't go to sleep until I "got saved." She said, "Let's wait until your father comes home, and we'll talk about it together."

Soon I heard my father's whistling as he walked home from church in the dark. My heart pounded with excitement because I knew that the moment of my salvation was nearing. Shortly we gathered in my parents' bedroom, and I shared again my desire to be saved. In moments we were on our knees. There at the end of my parents' bed, I trusted Christ and received the gift of eternal life.

I still have that scene in my parents' bedroom vividly etched in my mind. I remember looking out the window later that night and saying, "Lord, I believe I'm the happiest boy on the face of the earth." That joy and confidence are in my heart to this day, and they will only grow throughout eternity. Now, as a pastor, father, and grandfather, I have had the blessed privilege of sharing this testimony with my own children, grandchildren, and countless others . . . including you.

As the authors and compilers of this book, we at first felt awkward about sharing our testimonies with the others you will find on these pages. But every testimony is a reminder of God's "amazing grace" available to you . . . if you will simply repent and believe on Christ.

"I know whom I have believed, and am persuaded that he is able to keep that which I have committed unto him against that day" (2 Tim. 1:12).

62

BUILDING A
SHOESHINE BOX

Edwin Young

Chicago street kids came to Dwight L. Moody's class to get a nickel. Kids came to a Florida Sunday school to earn a goldfish. Ed Young came to Vacation Bible School to build a wooden shoeshine box, but God had a greater purpose. Let Ed Young share the story of what happened as he built a wooden shoeshine box.

————————————

When I was twelve years old, my mother wanted me to go to Vacation Bible School in my home church of Laurel, Mississippi. I told her that I did not want to go that year. As a twelve-year-old boy, free for the summer, I had better plans for my days than going to VBS! But one day one of my buddies asked me if I were planning to go. When I answered no, he urged me to go with him. He told me that all the boys were going to build shoeshine boxes as the craft activity. I really wanted to do that, so I told my mother that I'd had a change of heart and decided to go. Every day that week I walked to VBS at the First Baptist Church of Laurel, so I could build a shoeshine box.

The day before the decision service, our pastor's wife, Mrs. L. G. Gates, pulled me from a line to talk with me. I'll never forget the occasion. She said, "Edwin, you need to know Jesus," and she proceeded to share the gospel with me by using John 3:16. She led me in a prayer to receive Christ as my Lord and Savior. She also explained about going forward in church to make my public profession of faith and about believer's baptism. So in the VBS commencement service, I walked forward to let everyone know that I had received Christ—that I was "putting up my flag for Jesus." That following Sunday morning in the First Baptist Church of Laurel, Mississippi, I was baptized.

So there will always be a special place in this pastor's heart for Mrs. L. G. Gates and for Vacation Bible School. It's a great opportunity to reach kids for Christ!

———————————

It is a testimony of God's love for us that He often uses the things that interest us to confront us with the gospel message. How has God spoken to you through your "interests"?

"But Jesus said, 'Suffer little children, and forbid them not, to come unto me: for of such is the kingdom of heaven'" (Matt. 19:14).

63

DO YOU HAVE A TESTIMONY?

It was Thanksgiving, and the entire family was gathered for the traditional time of food and fellowship. Little did they know that they were in store for one of the most moving and stirring moments in their lives. Their father stood awkwardly at the head of the table, cleared his throat, and asked for their attention.

"You know," he said, "I have always said there are two things I would not discuss—religion and politics. And, about religion, I have always said that it is a personal matter. Well, I still believe that religion is personal. But lately I have come to understand that it was never meant to be kept private."

"On this sheet of paper," he continued, "I have written the testimony of my faith in Christ. I will admit that, until recently, I didn't have a testimony. That's why I didn't want to discuss it. But recently all that changed, and I want you to know about it. I'm a little new at all this, so if you don't mind I'd just like to read this to you."

In Their Own Words

A hush fell over the room as the father humbly read his testimony to his family. Unaware of what was happening, the father stumbled on through the brief statement of his faith. When he looked up he was amazed. Sons turned their faces toward the wall to hide the tears that were welling up in their eyes. His wife and daughters dabbed the tears that were now flowing down their cheeks. His grandchildren were looking in curiosity at their parents to determine just what was happening.

Little did that father know that he was setting in motion a series of events that would ultimately see all of his family members come to Christ. This would be a legacy that would be passed down for generations to come. And little did the family or the father know that they would gather once again only a few weeks later. This time it would be at a graveside where his earthly remains would be deposited with the clear assurance that he was with God.

Your Testimony

On more than one occasion, grief-stricken children have stood at the casket of their father asking, "Pastor, do you believe my father will be in heaven?" The pastor, of course, will try to comfort them, but he cannot give them the assurance they so desperately need. After all, the Scripture clearly states that one of the evidences of genuine salvation is a willingness to testify to that fact. The psalmist exclaims, "Let the redeemed of the LORD say so" (Ps. 107:2).

In the preceding chapters you have read the testimonies of men and women who are not ashamed to declare openly that they have come to Christ and just how it happened. Jesus said, "Whosoever therefore shall confess me before men, him will I confess also before my Father which is in heaven. But whosoever shall deny me before men, him will I also deny before my Father which is in heaven" (Matt. 10:32–33).

That clear and unequivocal statement by our Lord leads to the following questions:

- Do *you* have a testimony of personal faith in Christ that is clear, consistent with Scripture, and obviously evidenced today by the changes in your life?
- Have *others* heard about this relationship you have with Christ and seen the evidence in your life? Your answer to these questions will tell you whether you have experienced God's salvation at all—whether, in fact, you will spend your eternity in heaven.

Who Should Hear Your Testimony?

List names in various categories—spouse, children, parents, other family members, coworkers, friends, neighbors, your church, etc.

Write It Out . . . in Your Own Words!

Complete this form as a guide to your personal testimony of faith.

It's your testimony! Isn't it time others heard it? Why not go out and share it with someone . . . *in your own words?*

My Personal Salvation Testimony

I, _____, have the certainty that if I were to die today, I would spend my forever in heaven.

"These things have I written unto you that believe on the name of the Son of God; that ye may know that ye have eternal life" (1 John 5:13a).

If I were asked, "How can you be certain that you will spend your forever in heaven?" I would respond:

_____

_____

_____

_____

As best I recall, I repented of sin and accepted Jesus as my Savior at _____

_____

when I was _____ years of age. When I think about that important event, I remember:

_____

_____

_____

_____

_____

_____

_____

Since I received Christ, I can see God's hand at work in changing me and in equipping me for His service in the following ways:

_____

_____

_____

_____

_____

_____

Some of the people whom the Lord used to lead me to Christ:

_____

_____

_____

_____

_____

_____

Jesus said that true believers will openly confess their faith through scriptural baptism.

In Their Own Words

I was baptized at: _____

Approximate date: _____

Signatures:

_____

(My signature)

_____

(A witness who has read my testimony)

_____

(Pastor)

Epilogue: A Library Is Burned

The funeral was over. The casket had been lowered into the ground and was now disappearing under the red African clay, which fell upon it with a powdery "thump . . . thump . . . thump." Somber and teary-eyed family and friends were now drifting back toward their homes as the setting sun streaked the sky with brilliant colors. A missionary stood looking into the distance, trying to etch the moment in his memory. Next to him stood the old pastor, crumpled hat in hand, scuffing the ground with his shoes—his only shoes which were much like him, worn down with years of use.

Finally, the pastor broke the silence with a sentence—just one sentence filled with incredible wisdom. "We have a saying that 'when an old man dies, a library is burned.'" The missionary simply nodded in agreement. But now, years later, as the visual memories of that moment fade, that one sentence continues to impress its truth upon him. Indeed, when anyone dies "a library is burned."

As with any library, some volumes in the library of your own life are of greater value than others; some contain mere trivialities, while others record the "essentials." It was at another funeral, this one in a large and sophisticated downtown church in a major city, that I came to realize what is the most important volume in the library of life.

The crowd had been dismissed, and now the immediate family was gathered around the casket containing the "earthly suit" of their beloved husband and father. "Tell me, preacher," begged a sorrowing daughter. "My father is in heaven, isn't he?"

I don't remember exactly how I responded to the plea of that man's brokenhearted daughter. But I do remember thinking, *Why didn't she know? Why didn't he take the time to relate the experience (if indeed he had one) of his own personal conversion to Christ? After all, there is nothing I can say now that will change his eternal destiny. I can't preach him into heaven!*

This book has a distinctly twofold purpose: First, it is a public record of the testimonies of faith of men and women who have met Christ and want to tell about their personal experience of conversion. They are each giving you the opportunity to "check out" this important volume from their "library of life." You have the privilege of opening the pages of their diaries, pages that record in intimate detail the most important decision of life and its eternal consequences.

Second, it is our desire that you will also personally experience the amazing grace of God through faith in Christ. Then, like the people in these pages, it is our prayer that will go on record, unashamedly relating your own testimony of faith.

One day the library of your life will be burned; you too will be gone from this earth. That experience will probably not occur just when, where, or how you now imagine. The decision you make regarding Christ while in your lifetime will determine just where you spend your eternity. The psalmist urged, "Let the redeemed of the LORD say so" (Ps. 107:2 NKJV). And Christ bluntly stated, "Whosoever therefore shall confess me before men, him will I confess also before my Father which is in heaven. But whosoever shall deny me before men, him will I also deny before my Father which is in heaven" (Matt. 10:32–33).

Now is the time to go on record with the story of your own experience with Christ, told in your own words among your own family and friends. The very record of that experience will give you the opportunity to relive its wonder and refresh your commitment. So tell it . . . in your own words!

CONTRIBUTORS

John Bisagno—Pastor (retired), First Baptist Church, Houston, Texas; author and former nightclub entertainer.

Bill Bright—Founder and retired president of Campus Crusade for Christ, author, teacher, and speaker in virtually every country of the world.

Vonette Bright—Internationally known speaker respected for her leadership in the area of prayer and evangelism, working along with her husband in Campus Crusade for Christ.

Truett Cathy—Founder of Chick-fil-A, speaker, author.

Morris Chapman—Pastor, author, chief executive of the Southern Baptist Convention.

J. R. Church—Author, speaker, founder and president of "Prophecy in the News."

Forrest Claunch—Oklahoma State Representative.

William Crews—President of Golden Gate Baptist Theological Seminary.

William Wayne Bennett, Jr.—Former pastor of Central Baptist Church Jacksonville, Florida, author, and teacher.

YoYo Collins—Evangelist, author, and musician.

Charles Colson—Former U.S. presidential aide, founder of Prison Fellowship Ministries.

W. A. Criswell—Deceased, long-time pastor of First Baptist Church, Dallas, Texas, author, and Christian statesman.

Daniel Davis, Jr.—Veteran U.S. Marine Corp and evangelist.

James Dobson, Jr.—Noted radio personality, author, founder, and president of Focus on the Family.

Shirley Dobson—Speaker, leader in the National Day of Prayer, working closely with her husband in the ministry of Focus on the Family.

James T. Draper, Jr.—Former pastor, president of LifeWay Christian Resources, author, and speaker worldwide.

Jim Elliff—Founder and president of Christian Communication Worldwide, former pastor, author, and speaker.

Elisabeth Elliot—Former missionary, renowned speaker, and author.

Ken Freeman—Evangelist and author.

Leonard G. Goss—Editorial director for Broadman & Holman Publishers.

Bill Gothard—Founder of the Institute of Basic Life Principles, speaker, teacher, and author.

Michael Gott—Evangelist with a missions focus.

Charles Hand—Former associate to Dr. Jack Hyles at First Baptist Hammond, Indiana, pastor, and evangelist.

Stan Hannan—Evangelist, former chaplain in the Rhodesian army.

O. S. Hawkins—President of the Annuity Board of the Southern Baptist Convention, author, and former pastor.

Ken Hemphill—President of Southwestern Baptist Theological Seminary, author, and former pastor.

Jim Henry—Pastor of First Baptist Church, Orlando, Florida and author.

Rudy Hernandez—Evangelist, former pastor, and author.

Ron Herrod—Evangelist, former pastor, and author.

Junior Hill—Evangelist and author.

Johnny Hunt—Pastor of First Baptist Church, Woodstock, Georgia and author.

Jim Inhofe—U.S. Senator, Tulsa, Oklahoma.

Joe Kalil—Florida businessman.

Charles S. Kelley—President of New Orleans Baptist Theological Seminary, author and preacher.

Rick Kunz—Missionary in Argentina and former pastor.

Richard Land—President of the Southern Baptist Convention's Ethics and Religious Liberty Commission, author, and radio communicator.

Tim Lee—Veteran U.S. Marine Corp. and evangelist.

Natasha Matskevich—Christian in Eastern Europe.

Josh McDowell—Popular author, speaker, and evangelist.

James Merritt—Pastor of First Baptist Church, Snellville, Georgia.

R. Albert Mohler, Jr.—President of Southern Baptist Theological Seminary, author, and editorialist.

John Morris—President of the Creative Research Foundation, author, and teacher.

Jim Murray—Singer, evangelist, and former member of The Imperials.

Manuel Noriega—Former leader of Panama.

Sithon Nuon—Cambodian refugee and pastor of Cambodian church.

Stephen Olford—Pastor, evangelist, author, teacher, founder and president of Olford Ministries.

Ron Owens—Musician and composer.

Patricia Owens—Musician and composer.

H. Franklin Paschall—Former pastor of First Baptist Church of Nashville, Tennessee.

Paige Patterson—President of Southeastern Baptist Theological Seminary, former pastor, author, evangelist, and teacher.

Jerry Rankin—Former missionary and president of the International Mission Board of the Southern Baptist Convention.

Robert Reccord—President of the North American Mission Board, former pastor, and author.

Chip Reynolds—Assistant pastor, former gambler/nightclub owner.

R. Phillip Roberts—President of Midwestern Baptist Theological Seminary, former pastor, and author.

Darrell Robinson—Former pastor and head of the evangelism division of the Southern Baptist Convention Home Mission Board.

Adrian Rogers—Pastor of Bellevue Baptist Church, Cordova, Tennessee, author, and radio Bible teacher.

Bailey Smith—Founder of Bailey Smith Evangelistic Association, author, evangelist, and former pastor.

J. Harold Smith—Deceased, former pastor, evangelist, and author.

Ruffin Snow—Pastor of Tri-Cities Baptist Church, Conover, North Carolina.

R. C. Sproul—Founder of Ligonier Ministries, seminary professor, author, and radio Bible teacher.

John Sullivan—Chief Executive of the Florida Baptist Convention, former pastor, and author.

Jack Taylor—Conference speaker, author, and former pastor.

Mark Trammell—Founder of the Mark Trammell Trio and former singer with the Cathedrals.

Jerry Vines—Pastor of First Baptist Church, Jacksonville, Florida, author, and teacher.

Larry White—Pastor of the Deaf at First Southern Baptist Church, Del City, Oklahoma.

Robert Gee Witty—Founder of Luther Rice Seminary, author, teacher, and former pastor.

Tom Elliff—Pastor of First Southern Baptist Church, Del City, Oklahoma and author.

Edwin Young—Pastor of Second Baptist Church, Houston, Texas, and author.